# Recovering
# My True
# *Self*

MELISSA MAYER, DPT

**BALBOA**.PRESS
A DIVISION OF HAY HOUSE

Balboa Press books may be ordered through booksellers or by contacting:

Balboa Press
A Division of Hay House
1663 Liberty Drive
Bloomington, IN 47403
www.balboapress.com
844-682-1282

Print information available on the last page.

ISBN: 978-1-9822-4463-7 (sc)
ISBN: 978-1-9822-4465-1 (hc)
ISBN: 978-1-9822-4464-4 (e)

Library of Congress Control Number: 2020905787

Balboa Press rev. date: 04/28/2021

To my mom, for bringing me into this world so I could create and for the many sacrifices you made for me

# CONTENTS

# INTRODUCTION

There was a full moon on the evening of Sunday, December 3, 2017. I was sitting on the couch with my husband, Ken, when I involuntarily blurted out, "I want to write a book." The confused expression on his face was justified. I had never formally written anything before—especially not a book! I have a bachelor of science in marine science and a doctorate in physical therapy, and I had a limited background in the arts. I also had a restrictive belief about myself that I wasn't creative enough to be a writer. I didn't think I possessed the required language and grammar skills.

I had just turned thirty-seven. I was bursting with empowerment from a week of celebrations: hosting Thanksgiving at our home with our wonderful family, enjoying a luxurious and intimate birthday dinner with Ken, and ending the week at a dear friend's fabulous party. These events affirmed the sweet spot of contentment I was experiencing, an ease and flow that took thirty-seven years to achieve.

A month earlier, I had started reading *The Artist's Way* by Julia Cameron and had begun a consistent daily ritual of morning writing. The twelve-week self-study course had recommended the daily writing as well as weekly exercises aimed at personal growth. This had ignited a dormant creative spark within me and was becoming a cosmic road map before my eyes. That night as I looked at the brilliant light from the moon and made my declaration to Ken, the clarity I felt was profound—and it still is.

I went right to work that evening, and the euphoric feelings kept me up all night. The next morning, a Monday, was no ordinary manic Monday. Driving my kids to school, I was filled with excitement. I had a cosmic inspirational vision to write a book, and I wanted to shout it from the rooftops. Fortunately, a calmer voice inside my head was telling me to refrain. The inspiration to write was so far just a tiny seed of desire; it would need to be protected and nurtured in order to grow and stand on its own.

Still, desperate to be heard, and wanting some way to celebrate this moment, I did what I had often done to mark what felt like a deeply significant milestone: I got a tattoo. The tattoo artist drew the stencil freehand and inscribed the elegant script on my right forearm—*Synchronicity*. Psychologist Carl Jung introduced the concept of synchronicity to describe events that are meaningful coincidences. I had experienced the feeling of synchronicity many times, but I had never had a term to accurately describe it.

For the rest of December and into 2018, I slowly—without realizing it—began to undergo a preparatory process. It barely had a pulse, but, on some level, I could feel it. It was difficult to articulate to those around me that a path was unfolding before me. Through the writing in my morning pages—after I emptied my head of the thoughts of my day-to-day experiences—I could start to see past the annoying tediousness of errands, complaints about traffic, small talk, and scenarios where I felt like a victim.

As I waded through the words and cleared away what felt like illusion and ego, I began to identify with my faint inner voice—which seemed to be getting stronger and clearer every day. Years back, I had read Wayne Dyer's *I Can See Clearly Now*. In that book, the beloved American self-help author looks back on the events that have occurred in his life and does so with a clarity that only comes with the perspectives of time and experience. I can see now how perfect my own timing was. I continued my daily writing and blissfully began tinkering with ideas that would eventually lead to the book you are now reading. As it turned out, the writing I was doing was actually preparing me for the truly transformative opportunity that would come several months later. When it came, I was ready. The synchronicity was truly amazing.

In the spring of 2018, Ken and I discovered that, in a mere few months, we would be undergoing one of the most profound experiences of our lives. Although we had known for almost seven years that Ken was going to need a kidney transplant, we didn't know when he was going to need it. Ken had few symptoms or physical signs to help us gauge when the transplant might be necessary. Since he did not appear ill, and was not on dialysis, we rarely discussed the matter, and as time went by we filed the information in the back of our minds.

Ken was working full-time as the director of hospital medicine at our local community hospital. He felt strong and was able to meet the high demands his position entailed. The only indicator regarding the function of his kidneys was a raised blood level of creatinine. This chemical waste molecule rises in the blood due to poor clearance by the kidneys. Over the years we had watched this number rise from 2.0 to 5.0, indicating a slow failing of his kidneys. We were so blessed that these slowly rising blood levels were the only evidence, and that for all those years our life was unrestricted.

All of a sudden, the New York Presbyterian transplant team said it was time. Ken was frequently taking days off work and traveling to New York City for chest x-rays, blood work, stress tests and consultations to ensure he was healthy enough to have major surgery. I often accompanied him— since I also needed testing. Several years earlier, a handful of friends and family were tested to see if they were a match to give Ken a kidney. The best match was me. Without a doubt, I wanted to be the donor.

This book is an opportunity for me to look back and tell the story of the deeply transformative journey of recovering my true self. Regardless of its outcome, this book has brought so much joy, healing, self-expression and clarity into my life. I am so grateful for that. Even though I am a physical therapist by trade, I have always thought long and hard—many would say too long and too hard—about everything and anything. I started journal writing in high school. Writing was always there, when I allowed it to be, to help put the pieces of my life together in a poetic dance filled with fun and light—at least on a good day. Throughout the years, regardless of the path I was on or the multiple places I lived, writing in my journal has helped me make sense of the world and has calmed my soul. I like to think of this book not only as a chronicle of my transformational journey, but more importantly as an affirmation of gratitude for the life I have been fortunate enough to live thus far.

This is also a story about recovery in the various stages of my life: recovering from struggles I encountered while I was coming of age and finding my voice, discovering a deeper connection with my true self, recovering from giving birth and the transition into parenthood. It continues with recovery from struggles with food and alcohol, creative recovery, and recovering from donating my kidney to my husband—and the associated transformational journey.

I realize the word *struggle* is relative. There are various degrees of struggle, some more obvious and traumatic than others. I also realize we all have struggles, and minimizing them because they aren't as bad as someone else's is denying them and hinders a person's opportunity to transform. I respect the struggles of others. For many years, I fell victim to my smaller struggles, but after this most recent and larger struggle with Ken's kidney transplant—and my part in it—I realize how, taken together, they all have contributed to this opportunity for growth. I originally viewed the transplant as an obstacle; later, I saw it as an opportunity. As a result, I have been able to come to terms with, and let go of, so much that had been holding me back. I continue to evolve, and by deepening my connection to myself, find even greater happiness.

I have been on an epic search for happiness my whole life. Even though happiness may have been there all along, I often didn't see it or claim it. My childhood and early years make up the foundation of this story, but the transformative journey that is the heart of this book was really born in December 2017, shortly before I went to Sedona, Arizona. It was a vacation that came with great timing; the energetic red rock vortices were the perfect place for my vision to gain momentum and grow. Then, in January of 2019, a few months after the transplant, I got an incredible opportunity to travel to Sri Lanka with an amazing group of people from the Long Island Buddhist Meditation Center. We were accompanying a very accomplished monk who was invited back to his tropical island homeland by the president of Sri Lanka to honor him for his work spreading the philosophy and teachings of Buddhism. Self-growth can occur anywhere, but for me it tends to grow wings when I feel the freedom of traveling.

Many years of reading self-help books and listening to the stories of others inspired me to want to tell my own story. I hope this book will inspire and connect you to your story. This book fits into the self-help genre, but it is not intended to tell you how to live your life. I did include a toolbox at the end of the book to give you a nudge, if you are needing it. Ultimately, my prayer for you is that you go on your own journey of self-realization to discover the best version of yourself. If I can do it, I know you can too!

I thank you from the bottom of my heart for allowing me to share my work with you. I would like to close by saying *Namaste*. I believe the depth of this divine word transcends language. Still, I have heard *Namaste* translated in numerous satisfying ways. Here are a few:

- I bow to the divine in you.
- The deepest part of me acknowledges the deepest, the most honest and vulnerable, part of you.
- The light in me honors the light in you.

# CHAPTER 1

# Stepping Outside My Comfort Zone

I have a magnet on my refrigerator that states, "Life begins at the edge of your comfort zone." I have seen this quote from the American author Neale Donald Walsch on coffee mugs and stationery. Although it is commonly seen, I believe this notion can be a tricky point to navigate. Personally, it brings a feeling of butterflies in my stomach—which is a sign I always know I'm onto something. As Karen Salmansohn says in her book, *How to be Happy, Dammit*: "Your painful feelings equal your proud proof you are dealing with your life head on."

I don't seek out pain, at least not anymore. However, I do find a small amount of emotional discomfort reassuring. I like facing the music of my inner voice. At times—less often these days—I have drowned it out with countless forms of noise, only to quiet down and see that it is still there. I've come to embrace and befriend discomfort. It no longer scares me the way it once did. Negative mind chatter frequently creeps in, but because I am more deeply connected to who I am now, it no longer pulls the same weight.

I look at childhood pictures of me and see a happy baby and toddler. Love seemed abundant; I come from a family and extended family that unapologetically claims, "We are the best family." I would never negate that statement. My grandmother and great-uncle immigrated to New York City from Turkey in the 1920s. They survived the Armenian genocide, and like many others, they came to America looking for a better life.

In the 1940s, my uncle left the city for the nearby New Jersey suburbs to own property and move the family to a "safer" neighborhood. My grandmother married, had children, and stayed in New York. When my mother was eleven, her father passed, leaving my grandmother a single mother of three daughters. My mother recalls how her mother, at age forty-seven, left her and her two sisters in their Washington Heights apartment to travel downtown to her new job at the department store Lord & Taylor.

My mother's older sister, Madeleine, then fifteen—with occasional help from their grandmother—helped care for the home and my mother's younger sister, who was in preschool at the time. My grandmother eventually remarried and moved to New Jersey. My mother graduated from high school and soon met my dad at a dance in the next town over, where my dad had grown up. I lived in that town for the first decade of my life.

After my parents married, and shortly before my birth in 1980, my grandmother decided to move to Florida with her second husband and her two daughters. My mother decided to stay in New Jersey to raise her family. The initial heartache and feeling of abandonment when her family had moved was difficult for her to acknowledge and reconcile. Even so, it worked out for my little sister and me. We got to spend a month every summer swimming in Grandma's pool and going to Disney World—every child's dream.

My grandmother lost her second husband when I was in college. She passed a few months later after a tragic fall complicated by a massive stroke. Suddenly, within a few months, my mom and her two sisters were without parents. Seven years later, my mom's older sister was tragically murdered in the same Florida house that had contained so many wonderful memories.

My father too was no stranger to struggle. He lost his mother before the age of two and grew up without the unconditional love of a mother. His father did go on to remarry a woman who, unfortunately, treated him, by today's standards, abusively. Growing up my father never spoke ill of his stepmother, and even recalled how she cared for his father until his death from pancreatic cancer in 1985. My sister was also born in 1985, when I was 5 years old. That same year my father lost his brother to leukemia. Years later, learning this tragic timeline of losing his brother and father back to back, in addition to how he was treated by his stepmother, I am amazed by his resilience.

My dad was a third-generation general contractor. Although he and my mom had not come from much, they were able to literally build a solid foundation, live in nice homes, and become financially secure. When I was born, and throughout my childhood, my parents provided all of my basic physical needs and then some. As I grew older, I little by little learned of some of the earlier struggles my parents had faced, but living a very privileged upper-middle-class lifestyle in suburban New Jersey, I had no connection to those struggles. In fact, my parents had worked hard to give my sister and me a life without struggle.

As a parent now, I know of this need to try to prevent your child from struggling. It has taken me many years to understand that a lot of learning comes from these struggles. I wish my parents had been more forthcoming in sharing their struggles, how they felt during them, and what it took to overcome them. In hindsight, I realize that it might have been difficult to share and reflect on those feelings. As I started to transition from carefree childhood to adolescence, I started to experience my own struggles, the struggles of growing up that we all face. However, I didn't realize I had two resources living under the same roof who knew all about surviving struggle.

My adolescent struggles, fortunately, did not include the deeper hardships my parents' lives included. In comparison, my struggles while coming of age seem quite minor. However, I have learned denying and ignoring them is what made me have to go back many years later to heal them.

Friedrich Nietzsche said, "To live is to suffer, to survive is to find some meaning in the suffering." Initially, I felt guilty for naming my suffering. However, years later, when I did, I was able to find invaluable meaning in the form of clarity, wisdom and insight. Going through this process of healing allowed the realization that I myself was a healer. It seemed no coincidence that my personal experiences in healing allowed me to facilitate in the healing of others. I am grateful to those who helped open my eyes to a better understanding of this process. I have also seen that being an active participate in one's own healing is essential and imperative. I am humbled to now facilitate healing in others. I remind myself over and over that it is not my role to heal my patients. Rather, I try to help open their eyes, so they can heal themselves.

When I was nine years old, my parents bought a small farmhouse in a neighboring town and moved our family there. My dad built a grand addition, more than doubling the size of the old house. It was challenging for our family of four to live in the house during the transformation, but my parents made it work. The result was a gorgeous house on more than an acre of property—which was unusual in such a congested suburb.

Although the distance from the old address to the new one was a mere nine miles, the move felt significant. I didn't even realize how difficult that move in fourth grade was for me until I was thirty-seven. When I was reflecting with my mom, she said she had seen the toll it took on me, but my family was "moving on up" into a bigger home in a more upscale town which boasted of better schools.

The very next year, when I was in fifth grade, there was another move from the new elementary school I had barely gotten a handle on to a new middle school. I lovingly refer to this time as the adolescent jungle. This time I didn't even change houses or towns, yet as a young, highly sensitive child, it was disorienting.

I am certainly not alone in the struggles that middle school students face. It is a time chock-full of physical and emotional changes. I had few tools then to help me venture through this unsettling time. Of course, the struggles need to be put into perspective. All of my basic needs were met. My hardworking parents were married and loved me. I had lots of nice clothes on my back—my mom loves to shop—and I lived in a big beautiful home built by my extremely skilled father. Eventually, I made friends and survived. Looking back, it was a wise move for my parents to make, and I'm glad they did. This was the home I went back to for many years, and it is the town where I met my husband. It is always reassuring that the clock keeps ticking, and no matter what you are dealing with, things eventually start falling into place.

Every new school year and life transition felt harder for me to handle. Others around me simply seemed to move on, but I was very sensitive to change. Years later, I saw the diagnosis code on the top of one of my therapy progress notes: adjustment disorder.

In the meantime, I started to find my way, and before I knew it I was in high school. I started to move out of awkward preadolescence to a teenage life of driver's licenses, parties, and athletics. Competitive high school sports was a great opportunity to exercise growing muscles and gain new confidence. I was far from the fastest runner, or hardest hitter, but I held my own. I was thankful that I had started to get a small whiff of popularity, discipline, meaning, and teamwork.

Participating in competitive sports brought pressure, both externally from coaches and internally from myself. This physical transformation also came with continued struggles with my body image. High school trends and fashions looked great on tall and thin girls with blonde hair. I had brown hair, was five foot four, and a size twelve. I bounced between the various diets that were trendy at the time: high-protein diets like Atkins and South Beach, lemonade fasting, and crash diets. My aunt had even worked in a diet center in Florida and would ship me supplements and write out eating programs intended for me to "be healthy." Thankfully, despite my dissatisfaction with my appearance, I was healthy, reasonably strong, and even fairly coordinated. Looking back, I probably appeared well-adjusted. All in all I was, but I was a baby in respect to self-awareness. I felt a longing for it and thought about it a lot. I even started journal writing in an effort to connect to myself, but I quite often felt lost.

A little less than ten moves and many years later, as I sit in my current home, I still have the high school journals containing the writings of a young girl who seems foreign to me. The writing varies from calm confusion to screaming scribbles that I would write after coming home drunk from high school parties: wondering who I should date, why I was so different, and if there was anyone who would ever understand me. The butterflies in my stomach come back when I see how my inner voice was trying to come out and be heard but eventually turned into numbness. Ironically, it never occurred to me to pursue writing, yet here I am—almost twenty years later—realizing I did have a tool and a process that connected my head to my soul. I had developed a belief that a sensitive, introverted, intuitive, old soul of a girl wouldn't be socially accepted. In a subconscious effort to protect my vulnerability, I gave them a girl who liked the Yankees and Billy Joel and could do a keg stand.

Before I knew it, I was at my high school graduation and had a University of South Carolina sticker on the rear window of my 1989 black Nissan Maxima—the one that my parents had bought for me from our next-door neighbor. My high school guidance counselor had a personal bias in favor of South Carolina. My parents took me to visit USC, and the warm South Carolina sun did seem more appealing than the other schools I had visited in the Northeast.

I applied, was accepted, and before I knew it, was leaving home. I'm glad I clung to the opportunity to spread my wings and let it overpower my sensitivity to change. Breaking out of high school and being at a big university opened lots of doors, which was thrilling and scary. Of course alcohol was there again, as it had been in high school, as a reliable friend to help numb the fear, open social doors, and create new memories with my new friends. It was easy to see that I was lucky to have this opportunity to go away to school. I was glad I took advantage of it. That being said, I felt lost, as I was the first of my family to go away to college. I was in culture shock having grown up in New Jersey and was now going to SEC college football games with sorority girls saying "y'all". I was in a different place, yet the familiar uncomfortable feelings remained. They made me question what was wrong with me, and I felt guilty for those feelings. I had so much, yet I was lost in my head. *Who am I?* It felt like the thousands who attended the big university were dancing around me in a carefree euphoric paradise, living the college dream of freedom and partying. In contrast, I often felt like a rain cloud was over my head following me everywhere.

However, sunny, warm USC wasn't such a bad place to feel lost. I am a proud USC alumnus; it had a beautiful campus and provided all sorts of opportunities to find your niche. There were plenty of lighthearted fun college days, and the struggle brought much growth. Still, with all those hindering thoughts and feelings, it was hard for me to find it. Revisiting the campus more than a decade later really made clear that I had numbed those dark and uncomfortable feelings with alcohol. I am thankful I met a group of angels, in the form of girlfriends, who I keep in touch with to this day. I experienced the light with them, and it helped me out of those dark times.

Despite some of those dark times, I more than made the best of my time at USC. I participated in a summer session abroad in desolate and exotic Providencia. The island is located in the Caribbean Sea, east of Nicaragua and Costa Rica, yet it is owned by Colombia. We had a brief stopover in the sprawling city of Cartagena, and I can vaguely remember an evening of taking a taxi ride through cobblestone streets that were filled with lively people. It was such a profoundly different environment than I had ever seen.

We took a puddle jumper to the mountainous Caribbean island, and I logged more than fifty dives toward my marine science degree. It was always fun to claim that degree, but I never ended up using it professionally. The extra credits from my trip abroad earned me the opportunity to graduate a semester early. That was never my goal, but it worked out well since I was ready to move on. Undergrad life at USC was great; I got a taste of expansion in my mouth, but it was watering for more. USC was a good first step on my journey of self-growth, but I was soon ready for the next step—and, boy, did it come.

After I graduated college, I had no idea what was next. I returned home to New Jersey and worked as a substitute teacher for children with disabilities in the school district where my mother was employed. It was rewarding work, but my heart wasn't in it. I had experienced so much in the past three and a half years. It felt empty coming home after school, eating dinner at the same table I used to as a teenager, and sleeping in my old room with posters and pictures from fun times that now seemed gone.

It felt odd to return to a familiar place that now felt so different because I was different. Driving by my old high school and friend's parents' houses—that no longer housed them because they were still in college—I felt like a stranger in a town I had once thrived in. Again, all the change was hard. My stomach turns as I remember those feelings of discomfort that were almost unbearable at times. Luckily, I didn't dismiss those feelings, but I wanted to.

I stayed connected to my dreams of expansion, and, like a knight in shining armor, my cousin invited me to come to San Francisco and temporarily live with her. I was so excited for a new door to open up, but I was terrified at the same time. This time, I wasn't just leaving for college; I was leaving and not knowing when or if I was coming back. At the same time, I had been offered a permanent substitute position at the school where I was working. It would pay well, and I could live at home and save money responsibly—or I could go out west with zero plans. My parents, who worked hard to earn everything they had, urged me not to go, which was even harder. I had always valued their opinion, and to rebel, especially when I was so unsure, was one of the hardest things I ever did. Before I knew it, my childhood best friend and I were driving my Toyota Corolla out west, and I was moving to San Francisco.

The decision to go to San Francisco was the biggest step outside my comfort zone I had made thus far. It was thrilling, but I was twenty-one, and leaving home again was painful. Unlike going to college, this time leaving home felt for real. It was traumatic, terrifying, and almost masochistic. *Why are you putting yourself through this pain? You don't have to move to San Francisco.* Deep down, I knew I did.

As a kid, I was a good girl who listened to her parents—for the most part. I became a bit more rebellious in high school, but I more or less adhered to the status quo. As it turned out, I stayed in San Francisco for nearly a year before returning to New Jersey for graduate school. That step of leaving, even though I came back, was empowering and gave me new comfort in my skin. I came back as a new person (maybe not visible to anyone else but me). Overcoming the knots in my stomach and going into the unknown was a life-changing adventure.

Living in California had been unlike anything I had ever experienced. It was a whole new culture, so different from the New Jersey suburbs I had grown up in, or the southern culture I had lived in for three and a half years. The hilly streets, cable cars, and colorful Victorian houses felt like an urban paradise that celebrated nonconformity, diversity, and a style of alternative and bohemian living that was eye-opening. The people I met were edgy, unique, liberated, and kind.

I felt freedom in a way I never had. College had felt like pseudo freedom, but this was the real thing. Growing up, I was influenced by my father, who was an outside-the-box thinker. Here and there, I would experience little bits of nonconformity by going to yoga with my dad, embracing environmentalism, and opening to more liberal perspectives (even though my knowledge of it all was quite primitive at the time). Growing up in the suburbs of New Jersey and then college life in Columbia, South Carolina, these lifestyle choices made me feel like an outsider. For the first time in San Francisco, nonconformist living was the majority, not the minority. Progressive politics, doing yoga, and enjoying time in nature were basically assumed positions.

A great example is the annual Bay to Breakers footrace that starts at one end of the city at the San Francisco Bay and goes almost seven and a half miles to the Pacific Coast. I'll never forget watching it near my Oak Street apartment, which was close to the course. Everyone was talking about the race; it was established in 1912, and in 1986, it was recognized by the Guinness Book of World Records as the world's largest footrace with 110,000 participants. I was familiar with the New York Marathon, and I asked local people if it was similar. The response would come in the form of laughter and a statement: "Just go and see for yourself."

I expected to see a bunch of runners, but I was surprised to see the extravagant, colorful, and flamboyant costumes. There were groups of people on moving floats (some with kegs of beer) that looked like a parade, and participants running in the nude! It was a fun party-style atmosphere celebrating life, freedom, and diversity and was such a great example of the originality, acceptance, and anything goes mentality of San Francisco that I had come to love. Although I was not as extroverted as the people around me, I felt liberated and accepted in their presence. I only went that one time. Later, I heard that residents along the parade route claimed the event was getting out of hand. In 2009, several years after I was there, an official ban was placed on floats, alcohol, drunkenness, and nudity. Although the party changed, and people complained, the changes destroyed much that made the race a national treasure for most of the century, but you can't destroy the spirit. The elaborate costumes and eccentricities continue.

San Francisco living also came with some real hardships. The city's dot-com boom and subsequent bubble burst made living conditions hard for a girl in her twenties just starting out. Since the job market in general was bleak, finding a job that utilized my degree was pretty much impossible. Luckily, my cousin and her husband were able to connect me to two consecutive bartending jobs.

The next challenge was finding affordable housing on a bartender's budget. It was scary and tedious spending hours on Craigslist, wading through ads, and contacting strangers, but it was interesting to travel around the city, see different apartments, and meet all sorts of eccentric people—and I mean *all* sorts. There were groups of people sharing rented rooms, vegetarian kitchens, and people of mixed genders, ages, and sexualities all living together. It was again pushing me outside my comfort zone. Until now, my roommates had only been college girlfriends and my family. This was something entirely different.

All of this was further complicated by being in a long distance relationship with my now husband, Ken. He and I had gone to our senior prom together and started dating the summer before we left for college. To our surprise, our relationship persevered while going to colleges in separate states—South Carolina and Virginia—but now we were in an opposite-coast, long-distance relationship. Our relationship was a big piece of my comfort zone, and being apart was hard. I loved him and I was dedicated to our relationship, but I was young and paving a new path, which made things confusing. Could I be in a relationship with the guy from home as I was starting a new life on the opposite coast? I wanted the answer to be yes.

A few months later, he came out to California to live with me in the rented two-bedroom apartment I was staying in with two other roommates. Initially, I shared a room with a girl I met on Craigslist, and another roommate lived in the small adjacent bedroom. When the neighboring roommate moved out, the girl I shared my room with moved into the neighboring bedroom, which allowed Ken and I to share the bigger room overlooking Oak Street and the panhandle of Golden Gate Park.

It was fun living together in the Upper Haight neighborhood, which was a few blocks from the famous Haight-Ashbury intersection. The neighborhood was foreign to us both, but as the months went by, it became our first of many homes together—with our roommate of course. I fell in love with San Francisco. I wanted to stay forever, but the reality was our life was on the east coast where our families and friends lived. So, when I lost my job at PJ's Oyster Bar, and Ken's temp work ended with a broken copy machine, and we were both accepted to graduate school in New Jersey, it seemed clear the next step was at the University of Medicine and Dentistry of New Jersey (UMDNJ).

Returning to our Jersey roots felt different than the return home after college. This time, instead of feeling uncomfortable, Ken and I were excited to return to academia and pursue medical and physical therapy schools. After the freedom of California and our new love of urban life, we opted not to move in with our parents. Instead, we rented an apartment on the corner of Luis Munoz Marin Boulevard and Grand Street in downtown Jersey City. It was perfect: a beautiful renovated walk-up studio apartment with a loft and small outdoor deck, close to school and convenient public transportation to Newark—where the school was located—and New York

City. The view from the street was charming, and it had lots of character. It was great for our first home together after the thrifty and romantic living we had done in San Francisco. As we started our life together, the up-and-coming neighborhood felt symbolic.

I had come to realize that physical therapy would be a good career for me when I was volunteering and then working at a physical therapy office in downtown San Francisco. It fed my interest (and degree) in science, required empathy and compassion working with injured people, which felt natural for me, and drew from my earlier days in athletics. Unfortunately, at the same time, my dear uncle suffered a tragic stroke that resulted in paralysis of one side of his body. It was a very upsetting time for my family to see a man who loved to travel the back roads of life battling the frustration of trying to move his arm and leg in a way that was seamless before the stroke. My uncle and I were always close, but we got closer during this time. I enjoyed spending time with him while he got physical and occupational therapy in his subacute rehab gym. The recovery work of rehab and the goal of healing gave me hope and insight that this work would satisfy my soul. Up until that point, I had no idea what I wanted to do with my life, but it became clear that I was meant to facilitate healing in some capacity. To mark this milestone, I got a tattoo on the inside of my left ankle—the Chinese symbol for healer. Deep down, I had always felt I was a healer. Now I was claiming it.

I started to research PT schools, and I realized there weren't many schools that would accept my prerequisite college courses. Being a marine science major, I took science classes designed for that curriculum but wasn't required to take Biology 101 or 102. Most PT programs required this, but UMDNJ accepted my coursework and accepted me in a very fortuitous way. Ken, following his passion to study medicine, was also accepted to UMDNJ, which felt like a real sign that destiny was with us in moving back to New Jersey.

Life was going well for a while, but a year later I was at a crossroad again. Ken and I were living happily ever after, which made me uncomfortable. *Is this it?* I had pushed out of my comfort zone and expanded and was now back in New Jersey living a new and improved life and enrolled in a program that felt right, but it still seemed like I had a lot of growing to do. I had been with Ken since we graduated high school, and although I

11

was in love with him, I feared we had met each other too young and were limiting each other's growth. I broke up with him and moved out of our new home. I was devastated and confused. I cut myself off from the most unconditional love I had ever known, and again experienced the same masochism I had felt when I left for San Francisco. I thought: *You don't have to do this. It is okay to be happy and love someone even if you feel you are too young.*

Ken was devastated and had a difficult time understanding where I was coming from, which was reasonable because I didn't understand what I was doing either. Luckily, at the same time, I had an opportunity to move to New York City. My childhood best friend, and the guy I traveled across country with, was moving to a three-bedroom apartment in Morningside Heights and had one roommate but needed a third. I agreed to move in and commuted to PT school from Penn Station in New York to Penn Station in Newark.

Living in New York City opened amazing new doors. Reuniting with my childhood best friend and getting to know a new roommate who became a dear friend who is still in my life—as well as meeting a slew of new people—helped familiarize me with a city I had grown up less than eleven miles away from but rarely experienced. I felt like I was back in San Francisco. My eyes opened to a whole new world, and I loved it. I was also torn. I wanted to share this new world with Ken, but I was afraid I had ruined any chance of us having a future together. I wanted it all: Ken, PT school, New York City living, and exciting adventures. Was that too much to ask? I struggled with this question and my search for happiness as I tried to listen to my confused inner voice and need for freedom.

In a meeting with my academic advisor, I burst out crying. The professor sat there awkwardly, but calmly and said, "Do you need a referral for counseling?" At first I was insulted. I had just broken up with my boyfriend, and I was upset. Did that warrant counseling? Thankfully, my ego quickly let go, and I agreed. Feeling like I had nothing to lose (and it was free for students), I had my first therapy session.

Ruth, the licensed clinical social worker I saw, counseled graduate school students and was insightful and profoundly helpful in organizing and managing the millions of thoughts and emotions going on inside of me. I was in my twenties, working toward my doctorate in physical therapy, trying to find my way in life, feeling very confused, and pushing away love.

When I opened up and exposed my vulnerability, Ruth sat there calmly and didn't look horrified. I had always tried to hold everything together. I had been afraid to reveal any darkness except when it was too bottled up and would come exploding out. I thought I was a mess and that going to therapy was admitting I had problems. Thankfully, Ruth saw my light and helped steer me back on course. She referred me to the teachings of Eckhart Tolle and his book, *Practicing the Power of Now*. I will never forget coming across the first page of this well-known book:

> The beginning of freedom is the realization that you are not "the thinker."
>
> The moment you start watching the thinker, a higher level of consciousness becomes activated.
>
> You then begin to realize that there is a vast realm of intelligence beyond thought, that thought is only a tiny aspect of that intelligence.
>
> You also realize that all the things that truly matter—beauty, love, creativity, joy, inner peace—arise from beyond the mind.
>
> You begin to awaken.

Seventeen years later, I still have the book, and when I read this passage now I still feel the freedom in it. It helped me understand that my fears are just thoughts; they aren't me. Since adolescence, I had identified with my thoughts. This freedom and awakening that I didn't have to live in the shadows of my thoughts changed my life.

I went on to read *Silence Speaks* and have followed Tolle's work, in some capacity, ever since. It began my New Age education and opened the door to realizing there was an entire genre of books and community of people dedicating their lives and work to the field of inner growth, self-help, and metaphysics. I remember my father referring to Deepak Chopra and going to yoga classes with him, which supported some of these philosophies. I'm grateful for this exposure from my father, as it helped me become familiar and comfortable with these ideas. These exciting new discoveries and my first experience in therapy led to an inner shift. The famous saying 'When the student is ready the teacher will appear' by Buddha Siddhartha Guatama, was evident here. These experiences helped me transition from a lonely lost soul to a student of self-exploration.

On the whole, working with Ruth was a wonderful process that brought clarity and wisdom. It helped me realize I wanted more than anything to be happy but didn't understand why I wasn't. I'll never forget confessing my deepest fear: "What if I am successful and married and find that I was never truly happy?" Ruth responded by suggesting I give myself permission to be happy. It sounded like such a therapist thing to say, but I am so grateful for that simple but profound advice. I realized I didn't have to fear the acquisition of happiness because it was born in me and was my right to claim at any moment. External situations—relationships, housing conditions, and exotic adventures—were what my soul was seeking, but, in my heart I was happy with who I was without any of it.

I can articulate this so clearly now. My happiness is no longer in question. At the time, the clarity was just born and was still a bit frail. Thankfully, when I expressed all of this to Ken, he took me back. Ken moved into my bedroom on 105th Street. I moved from sorrow to bliss. Neither of us had a job, I was still in PT school, and Ken was still in medical school, but we were young and in love. We lived in one of the best cities in the world and had exciting memories behind us and an unlimited future before us. It felt like we had it all.

We were living in an urban oasis with all sorts of exciting people around us. Ken and I were on the road to becoming health care professionals and were meeting people from all over the country (and the world) who were trying to make it in New York in entertainment, fashion, and business. It was scary at times living in what felt like a jungle with cold, harsh, fast-paced, cutthroat people trying to survive. As scary as it was, I also felt safe and at home. I made wonderful new friends but was often intimidated by all the exotic people I was coming into contact with.

I would see a wide variety of young talented designers, singers, dancers, actors, and more. These gifted souls were struggling to make it, and their freedom and self-expression fascinated me. I didn't realize it at the time, but I secretly longed for my own artistic gift. I had never acknowledged myself as a creative person. My last few years were in a world of academia and clinical experiences, which encouraged professionalism. I was thankful I had my aspiring career as a PT, but to some degree I also felt lame and sterile.

Before I knew it, I was offered a job at New York Presbyterian-Columbia Hospital. It was my first PT job and a wonderful sense of accomplishment after three long years of hard graduate school work. It also came with a much-needed paycheck. Even though I was saddled with student debt from paying rent and living off of my student loans, I pay them every month and still think it was worth every penny!

I also followed up on accomplishing a longtime goal of completing my two hundred-hour yoga teacher training and started returning to my love of holistic healing studies. Although I was proud of my new job and my career path, I knew from the beginning that a traditional health care environment was not right for me. However, I also knew I needed a full-time job with a paycheck, benefits, and experience before I could find my own nontraditional path in health care.

Ken and I were in a new phase. I had an exciting new career as a PT in New York City, and he was placed in a medical residency program at St. Luke's Roosevelt Hospital, only eight blocks north of where we were living. The residency even came with resident housing across the street from the hospital. We moved out of our shared apartment to our own one-bedroom apartment in an elevator building on 113th Street. Life was good. We had an elevator to move our boxes and furniture versus our old building, which was a walk-up, and we even now had a doorman! On New Year's Eve, we got engaged in Costa Rica, and the following November were married at Gurney's Inn in Montauk, New York. And to top it off, two months later, I was a newlywed off to India.

During my first year working as a physical therapist at Columbia-Presbyterian, a colleague had given an in-service on her experience with Health Care Volunteer Overseas (HVO), an organization that sends health care workers to various sites around the world. The health care workers provide continuing education to the local staff. As I heard my colleague share her impactful trip to a developing country, I was hooked instantly. I thought, *One day, that will be me.*

However, I was just settling into my new career, and with the start of student loan repayment and Manhattan rent, I couldn't go at the time. I changed PT jobs a few times, and five years later, I was filling out forms and interviewing over the phone. I was placed at Christian Medical College (CMC) in Vellore, India. Ken was very supportive, and even though we had only been married for two months, he said being married didn't mean saying no to my dreams. We even made plans to meet in Thailand after my trip for a formal honeymoon.

I had grown up on the East Coast, went to college in the Southeast, have driven cross-country twice, lived and traveled along the West Coast, and was now living and working in one of the biggest cities in the world. I felt I was starting to get a handle on things. I had traveled outside the country a few times, mostly to the Caribbean and my college abroad in South America, but traveling to the other side of the world and living in India for a month blew my mind.

I quit my job at an outpatient clinic on West Seventy-Second Street to volunteer for the trip. I had to pay for my flight, but my lodging costs were minimal. Ken was still a resident, so funds were tight, but I figured it would be an adventure on a budget. I packed my traveler's backpack and was surprised when I boarded my flight on the luxurious Etihad Airways. The lavish feel of traveling across the globe and the modern, upscale feeling of the layover in Abu Dhabi did not prepare me for the uneasiness I felt when I arrived at the Chennai airport.

In India, the fatigue of flying more than sixteen hours and my white skin being in the minority, my excitement converted to distress. I was a lonely stranger in a strange land, and my Blackberry did not work. It was before free Wi-Fi in terminals, and I was at the mercy of my earlier email correspondences in hopes of finding where to go and what to do next.

Luckily, the passenger who had been in the neighboring seat saw me wallowing about and showed me where to change money and get my bags. I went to the baggage claim and saw my yoga mat, which had broken free of my backpack, alone on the luggage carousel. Before long, my pack showed up too. I was way outside my comfort zone, but I was getting by.

Now I had to tackle transportation. Yikes! The emails had been unclear as to what to expect when I arrived. It was 4:30 a.m., and I was a volunteer health care worker. Did I really expect to be treated like royalty with a driver with a sign to be waiting for me at that hour? As it turned out, I walked to the nearby exit and Mr. Sukumar was standing there like a knight in shining armor! He put his arm around me and quickly escorted me past the alarming sea of humanity and into his cab.

I placed a lot of trust in Mr. Sukumar. He was the only person I knew for more than eight thousand miles, and I made the decision to deepen that trust when it came to him driving me a little more than eighty-six miles to Vellore. That was when I was first exposed to the road conditions in India. I was silently screaming when I saw how every traffic law and road condition I had ever learned was violated. The driving was a free-for-all, but trying to maintain some sense of brave faith in my new acquaintance, I stayed calm and tried to enjoy the almost three-hour ride. I stared out the window at the foreign but beautiful landscape, local people, and lots of cows—with painted horns and bells!

At seven thirty, we pulled up to the Modale Mani International Student Hostel. It was a little less than four miles away from the bustling town of Vellore, where the hospital was located. The campus was quiet and secure. It was gated and had been built just three years prior. Despite it being fairly new, it felt very similar to my dated college dorm at the University of South Carolina. However, I was told it was the nicest place for students and volunteers to stay. Regardless of the occasional small chameleon and sterile feel of the hostel, I was grateful. Unlike many of the other facilities on campus, we had a regular shower instead of a bucket shower in our rooms. An added bonus was the switch to turn on the small water heater for a hot shower. Although the conditions felt rough for an American, they were luxurious conditions for the majority of the country. My roommate was a student from the University of Kansas, and the hostel was filled with other students from the United States, Holland, Australia, and beyond.

Once I saw the other volunteers who were familiar with the culture, local currency, and with riding to the hospital on the bus, my previous alarming feelings felt a little silly. Before long, I was in that group and was experiencing exciting adventures in life beyond my comfort zone. I stayed there for twenty-three nights and paid 7,100 rupees ($154).

After I departed Vellore, I traveled solo on an overnight train to an ashram on the southern tip of India. Once again, I was outside my comfort zone, but I felt stronger because I had been in India for three weeks. Now, I was on a mission to experience yoga while I was in India.

Despite how hard I looked, in the three weeks I had been there, I hadn't come across a single yoga studio. I had come to learn that India is a very big country with all sorts of regional differences. I had spent my time in the state of Tamil Nadu, in a small Christian pocket where missionaries established the Christian Medical Center. I did go on weekend excursions to other parts of Tamil Nadu and learned that there were many different religions and languages even in just this one region.

I took the train to an ashram in the more tropical and green southern state of Kerala. I then flew north to Delhi, which brought another completely different regional experience. I ended my trip to India by seeing the beautiful, yet chaotic, Taj Mahal, which was the only thing I had known about India prior to traveling there.

I went to the Delhi Airport to leave India and reconnect with Ken. We hadn't seen each other in a month, and it was only three months since we were married. I missed him so much and was incredibly eager to see him and share my adventures. Without working cell phones, it was hard to connect. I knew his flight itinerary and was desperate to see him. I went to the Continental Airlines counter and asked where the passengers were from the Newark flight.

The airline representative said Ken was a layover passenger and didn't have a visa to be in India. He was with the other passengers in a special holding area, and I couldn't see him. I begged and pleaded and refused to give up. I continued my search until I finally found him in the hallway. My eyes filled with tears, and I ran to him and hugged him tight. It was one of the happiest and most romantic moments of my life! I already knew he was the man I wanted to spend the rest of my life with, but in that moment, it had never felt so right. Being together verified everything.

My trip to India had opened my eyes to so many other ways of life, poverty, beauty, survival, and contentment. I met people from all walks of life. There were often language barriers, but I would usually understand the question, 'Are you married?' and the follow-up question, 'do you have children?' With the language barriers—and the strong family values of the people I met—it was difficult to explain that I wasn't sure if or when I would be ready to have a family. After my time in India something shifted in me, and it became very clear to me that it wasn't a cliché tradition to have a family; it was a blessed privilege. It made me realize, I too wanted to partake in the joy.

In the Delhi airport, I was reminded of the song Ken and I danced to at our wedding: "You're My Home" by Billy Joel. The song states, "Home is just another word for you." Although we were far from home, I felt at home in Ken's arms. For the next ten days, we didn't leave each other's sides and had a fabulous honeymoon in Thailand. This had been a trip of a lifetime, and I was so glad I had the courage to take it! It was an extraordinary experience for an ordinary girl from New Jersey. Overcoming those early struggles helped lay the framework for continued transformation, and helped strengthen my roots so that when the winds came, my tree was strong enough to withstand them.

My trip to India was a little more than ten years after I graduated from high school. I had come a long way from the awkward, introverted, uncomfortable adolescent and teenager I was. College, physical therapy school, living and working in New York, getting married, and traveling to India made me feel so blessed and empowered. I couldn't believe so much had happened in ten years. I am so glad I stepped outside my comfort zone in each stage along the way, consistently moving past my own resistance to begin this journey of reclaiming my true self.

# CHAPTER 2

# Creative Parenting, Creative Recovery

After our return home from Thailand and India, Ken and I were living happily ever after in Manhattan. Ken was in the last year of his residency at St. Luke's/Roosevelt, and I started a new job working for a home care agency: the Visiting Nurse Service of New York. I was working near our apartment on West 113th Street and treating patients in their homes on the Upper West Side. I felt like I had it all: a great job, a great marriage, and my free spirit. By the fall, I was pregnant. It was a little less than a year since we had been married, but after being together for more than a decade, it felt like the right time.

Ken took the employee shuttle from Uptown St. Luke's Hospital to their downtown partner Roosevelt Hospital to meet me at the midwife's office for my first prenatal appointment. We chose this practice because they delivered babies at one of the cities' few natural birthing centers, coincidently located at Roosevelt Hospital, where Ken was employed. The office was conveniently located around the corner from Roosevelt Hospital on West 57th Street. We were sitting in the waiting room eagerly waiting to hear the heartbeat of our first child.

Besides the anticipation, I could tell something else was on Ken's mind. He'd had a kidney condition since childhood, and he had an appointment earlier in the day at New York Presbyterian with a new nephrologist. As we waited, I asked how the appointment went. He said that we were there for the baby, and he didn't want to talk about it at that moment.

Our appointment time passed, and we continued to wait. I grew impatient and demanded to know what had happened earlier. Finally, he told me that he would need a kidney transplant. I thought, *He seems so healthy. Why now?*

Ken said his new doctor wanted him to start the transplant evaluation process, which included getting a group of friends and family tested to see if they were a match. A living, willing donor would result in the best outcome.

As shocking as this news was, we continued with our appointment. I asked my midwife and the doctors at Columbia if I could get tested while I was pregnant, and the answer was yes. A few weeks later, I went with a few family members and a friend to get our blood drawn and waited for the results. We were grateful that we, so quickly, found so many people who were willing to participate.

When we got the results back, Ken's sister and I were matches. I wanted to be the donor, but with my pregnancy and not knowing the timing, we agreed I would be the donor and his sister would be the backup. Since we had a willing donor, Ken's nephrologist said we could put the process on hold. He also said we would need to monitor his blood work every three months and keep our fingers crossed to see how long we could go until the transplant was more critical. As it turned out, we were very lucky; we would have more than seven years until it was time. We resumed our daily life and filed the information in the back of our minds.

Before I knew it, I could no longer ride my bike to work, because my rapidly growing belly was getting in my way. I started taking the subway and the bus. I would drag my rolling book bag with my necessary home care gear to various apartments from Riverside Drive to Central Park West, from West Ninety-Sixth Street down to West Sixty-Sixth Street. Spring came and covering this big area and climbing four flights of stairs to treat patients, who lived on the top floor of their walk-up building, was getting tougher.

Working, pregnancy fatigue, adjusting to this new era of my life, and news of Ken's kidney was a lot. To top it off, I was waking up in the morning with itchy red bites on my body. Approaching my third trimester of pregnancy, I was already becoming more physically uncomfortable, and now these itchy bites made me incredibly uncomfortable in my own skin.

Ken was working long hours as a resident and did not have as many bites, so the problem fell mainly onto my shoulders. I took action, went to my doctor, and got the diagnosis I suspected but dreaded to hear: bedbug bites! I worked in various privately owned, rented, and public housing buildings, and I had picked them up somewhere along the way. I felt so helpless and vulnerable.

I felt like curling up in my mother's lap and crying, but I was about to become a mom. So, as helpless and disheartened as I felt, I had to step up. I did some research and hired an eco-friendly extermination company—I didn't want harmful chemicals around while I was pregnant. I got a new bed, dragged bags and bags of clothing to the coin-operated washers and dryers in the basement of my building, and finally resolved the situation. It was expensive and frustrating, and I still cringe when I think about it. At the time, I told almost no one due to the terrible stigma that comes with bedbugs. Later on, I discovered many other people I knew who had also gone through this trying situation and concealed it. Like many hard times, it does make you stronger. I suppose this is what gives a person, and a book, content.

Two weeks before my due date, I stopped working and spent my days walking, resting, washing, folding, and organizing baby gear. I eagerly awaited the birth. I was going to acupuncture, walking miles in the park, eating spicy food, and doing all the other tricks recommended to bring on labor. None of them worked, and my due date came and went.

A week later, my midwife informed me I wouldn't be able to deliver at the birthing center due to the hospital policy of overdue mothers being considered high risk. My midwife said the baby and I were fine, but if I really wanted to deliver in a cozy birthing center atmosphere, I could try a castor oil induction to help bring on labor.

I was so exhausted from the long pregnancy, and being overdue, that I agreed to ingest the vile castor oil. Well, it worked. The gastrointestinal stimulant had me almost immediately in the bathroom. A few hours later, I was on my way to the birthing center. I was relieved to finally be having my baby. The relief faded as my labor lasted all night and into the early morning. After 20 long hours of unmedicated labor, I was not progressing. The irony/catch 22 was upsetting. I had taken the castor oil to bring on labor so I could deliver naturally in the birthing center, but instead I had to be transferred upstairs to the maternity floor to get Pitocin to speed up the labor.

Old reliable Pitocin worked, and with the final surrender and acceptance of an epidural—and after almost two hours of pushing—we finally met Eliza Clementine Mayer. It was one of the happiest moments of our lives. She was healthy and beautiful and started to nurse almost instantly.

Childbirth was one of the most humbling experiences I had ever had. I wanted a natural birth, and like many mothers, I can attest that birthing rarely goes the way you plan it. Looking back, I wish I had been a little more patient and not taken the castor oil. I believe ingesting the oil, putting my body into labor before it was ready, resulted in the stalled labor. I have no way of knowing what would have happened, but if I had let go of my attachment to the natural birthing environment, would the outcome have been different?

Nevertheless, I am grateful the baby and I were healthy. I was able to have a vaginal delivery, and I did not require a cesarean section. However, the hours of pushing in a supine position, because I had an epidural and couldn't move around, had another consequence. Despite being a PT, I had never heard of a pubic symphysis separation after giving birth. So, I was surprised to hear this diagnosis from my midwife when I reported severe pain in my pelvis and difficulty walking. This coupled with the usual stresses of being a new mom—sleepless nights and long days caring for an infant—was rough. Rolling in and out of bed was painful and debilitating. This was unfortunate because every two hours during the day and night, I needed to nurse the baby, which required getting in and out of bed. Co-sleeping, and support from my family, helped me get through this challenging time. Thankfully, four to six weeks later the pain in my pelvis fully resolved.

A month later, Ken completed his residency and since our apartment was only for residents, we needed to move out. Eliza was just over a month old, and I was still adjusting to motherhood, recovering from the birth, and still up every two hours all night nursing. We decided to temporarily move into the house I grew up in and we spent the summer and fall living in New Jersey around family and friends, which was a big help. Ken commuted to New York where he continued at St. Luke's as an attending physician.

By February, Eliza was nine months. We were ready to move back to New York, and I would return to my job at the visiting nurse service part-time. We found a two-bedroom duplex on 105th Street, half a block away from my first New York apartment. I was excited to return to my old neighborhood, but it was an unpleasant surprise when we were robbed the first night we were back.

It was Super Bowl Sunday, and we went downtown with the baby to a friend's apartment to watch the game. We were very fortunate we weren't home when it occurred. When we came home that night, we noticed many of our electronic items missing, including our laptop computer, which had pictures of Eliza as a baby, my trip to India, and many other fond memories. The perpetrator entered the apartment through the fire escape window and into the room we were setting up to be Eliza's room. Looking at the crib against the fire escape window, which did not have a window gate, was upsetting and confusing.

My roommates and I had been robbed at our apartment on 105th Street, and my car was broken into while parked on 105th Street. I got over both instances quickly; I figured life in New York came with crime, and as long as I wasn't hurt, I could move on. This was different. We had a baby now, and I questioned if raising her in New York City was the right thing. I loved life in New York and figured my children would too, but this had shaken me up. I felt helpless and vulnerable, as I had in the bedbug incident, and called the management company to get them to install the thousand-dollar fire escape window gate that needed to open in case of a fire. They finally agreed to split the expense with us, and we continued living there with an improved peace of mind once windows were more safely secured.

Before I knew it, I was dragging my rolling home care bag again. This time, it had the extra weight of my breast pump. Fortunately, I had a wonderful pair of friends who let me pump at their apartment, which was conveniently located on the Upper West Side near my patients' apartments. It was challenging to find an appropriate place to pump on the streets of Manhattan, so I was grateful.

Life in New York was different. I was living on the same block as when I first moved to New York after my breakup with Ken. Only now, I was a working, pumping, New York mama. I questioned our long-term plan, but life was so busy I didn't have the luxury of time to contemplate it. I just went with it.

More change came with Hurricane Sandy hitting New York City that October. Downtown was flooded, and many people were without power. I had a feeling I was pregnant again, but the nearby Duane Reade wasn't open due to the storm and associated power outages. When the power came back, I purchased a pregnancy test. I was, indeed, pregnant again. Eliza was a year and a half, and I was still breastfeeding. I had heard you couldn't get pregnant when you are breastfeeding, but the stick with the red line indicated I was. Although it was a bit of a surprise—and sooner than we planned—in the back of my mind, I was hoping to get another childbirth in before the transplant. That part was good, but this pregnancy turned out to be much rougher. During my first pregnancy, I would come home after work exhausted but relieved to put my tired legs up. Now, I was coming home to a one-and-a-half-year-old. I was still up at night nursing. The sleepless nights and first trimester were rendering me an emotional wreck. I had to stop nursing.

My twenty-week anatomy scan had revealed a two-vessel cord, a mainly benign anatomical variation occurring in 1–1.5 percent of pregnancies. Although only having two blood vessels in the cord instead of three rarely affects the baby, this meant more prenatal visits and more monitoring. It was tedious finding childcare and scheduling my patients around more visits in order to sit on a fetal monitor and get more ultrasounds.

All this excessive testing gave the radiologists more opportunities to find more issues. This time, it was placenta accrete—the placenta growing too deeply into the uterine wall—placing me in a high-risk category. Being healthy my whole life and having a completely normal pregnancy with Eliza, I was 100 percent convinced this baby inside me was healthy. I thought all this unnecessary testing was leading to more problems, and the stress was taking a toll on me mentally and physically.

On the next visit, another radiologist found no evidence of placenta accrete and took me out of the high-risk category. I was a bit annoyed at what seemed like a misdiagnosis and the associated stress. Ken grounded me with his simple and pragmatic responses. When I told him I didn't have the condition, he said that was great, and we focused on the relief and validation that the baby and I were healthy. Feeling like I was living in a day-to-day survival mode, it was way more productive to listen to my inner knowing and simply move on.

I continued working through the winter and spring, and by June, I felt done. I was due in a month and had started to wear compression stockings to help relieve varicose veins and the heavy feeling in my legs, because I was on them all day. Then the summer heat came on, and I couldn't comfortably wear the compression stockings. One evening, I came home and collapsed on the couch. My legs felt like tree trunks, and I told Ken I could not work anymore. I hated to admit I couldn't do it all, but I surrendered and stopped working a month before my due date. It was a relief to stop working, but the fear of being a full-time caretaker set in.

As challenging as it was, I had enjoyed the balance of three days working and four days at home. I liked earning income, being a healthcare professional again, and the break from entertaining a toddler all day. Ken worked twelve-hour days—seven days on and seven days off—at the hospital. The weeks he worked equaled long days at home. I was in the last trimester of my pregnancy and hoped I could handle the demands of around-the-clock child care. As I contemplated my fear, I realized this was an opportunity. This was a career change. As much as I had enjoyed my work, being home all day with my daughter was a gift to be enjoyed and not a problem to be solved. I tried to survive as best I could by balancing frequent prenatal visits, caring for Eliza, and resting if possible.

My weekly appointments and frequent sonograms revealed another new problem: the baby had suddenly flipped into a breech position. I couldn't believe another issue had come up! I learned babies can flip while in utero and flip back. However, after thirty-five weeks, it becomes harder for them to flip back since the growing baby runs out of space.

Upset but still hopeful about having as natural a birth as possible, I did every bridging and any other exercise that people and the internet would recommend to flip the baby back. On occasion, I would get out to the Hamptons and spend lots of time swimming in the bay. The freedom of movement, the buoyancy and the salt water felt therapeutic.

I also scheduled an external cephalic version (ECV) to turn the fetus from a breech position to a head-down position. I went in on the morning of the procedure having had nothing to eat—at thirty-seven weeks— because the procedure, which has a 58 percent success rate, can also result in an emergency C-section. They prepare you as if you are having one. I was getting quite irritable not eating and facing the unknown, yet it was a miracle. The ECV was successful in flipping the baby. I had headphones in my ears, listening to Zen music and meditating.

The doctor put her two hands on my belly and said, "This may feel a bit uncomfortable." After a quick maneuver, she looked surprised and exclaimed, "Wow—that baby turned very easily."

Ken and I celebrated by having a big lunch at a Greek restaurant across the street. We were back on track in the non-high-risk bracket with our plan for a vaginal birth.

I was literally sweating out the last weeks of pregnancy in late June and early July. I had gone past my due date again. I pushed Eliza in a stroller every day to the neighborhood playground.

On July 8, I was at a prenatal appointment with the midwife. After the castor oil episode with Eliza, I told the midwife I was determined to go into labor on my own. She thought it would be soon and performed a "sweep" or stripping of the membrane. She said it wasn't inducing the way castor oil or Pitocin does, but it was a gentler assist to bring on labor. It worked, and I went into labor that evening. By two o'clock in the morning, Madeleine Margaret was born.

Madeleine was the name of my mother's sister who had passed several years ago. We chose the name in the hope of restoring love to a name that was tarnished by pain, and it really has! Margaret is also my middle name and was the name of my father's mother who died when he was a small child. It is also the name of my father-in-law's late mother. It was a perfect fit all around for the beautiful new girl in our lives.

I was so glad I had stayed true to my inner knowing that my baby was perfectly safe inside me all along. My pregnancy had been unnecessarily dramatic, but the birth was smooth. I felt like she slid right out of me. Thank goodness my pelvis had not separated again and stayed strong. I was able to walk out of the hospital without pain. With all of the complications during the pregnancy, there wasn't the option of the birthing center, but it hadn't mattered. I had let go of my preconceived notion of a natural birth and did the best I could. It was a great birth and didn't come with any what-ifs. The quick, smooth labor also came with a much easier recovery— maybe due to having ingested the prepared placenta smoothies made by my postpartum doula when I got home.

A week after the birth, I was back on the neighborhood playgrounds with two babies. Surviving life with two children was exhausting but empowering. I started to get into a rhythm. I realized it was the most meaningful work I had ever done. Yes, I helped patients as a PT in various capacities, but carrying my newborn in a baby carrier and watching my thriving two-year-old running up slides and exploring the many playgrounds we would go to, made me so proud of the family I was creating. It gave me a newfound respect for motherhood. I would see the other mothers and caretakers on the playgrounds and it felt like we were all connected by the common goal of doing the best we could for the children we were caring for. We shared safety concerns about our children, the need to get them outside (and kill time), and the struggle of telling a child it was time to go home when the child clearly didn't want to go. What neighborhood you were from, your profession, or your race didn't matter. We were all caring for children in Manhattan in our own unique ways, but at the same time we were united, even if we didn't have time to speak to each other. I noticed the wide variety of caretakers, from mothers, to nannies, to the occasional father, or grandparent. Only in New York City did such a wide variety of socioeconomic backgrounds exist on one playground. I was fascinated to see how, in a few short blocks, the landscape would change drastically. And then one of my children would spit up, cry, need a nap, or need to be fed—and it was back to work.

That September, Eliza was two and a half and at the appropriate age to attend a parent-child class at the Rudolf Steiner School. Eliza and I would take the M4 bus to East Seventy-Ninth Street and Fifth Avenue to the walk-up/brownstone building that served the younger children. Ken, my mother-in-law, or my mother would stay with Maddy who was two months old.

It was a very exciting time for me. My daughter was beginning her educational journey, and we could share it together. My cousin had introduced the concept of Waldorf education to me, and after a bit of resistance and way more research, I was excited to finally be experiencing it. Eliza and I walked upstairs to a small auditorium that was set up with natural wooden toys, hanging silk tapestries, and three teachers who spoke sparingly. They smiled warmly and invited us in.

The children were invited to play in the simple wooden toy kitchen and iron on a play wooden ironing board that was set up in front of an actual one where the teacher was ironing and softly humming. Another teacher was cutting apples and had a station set up for children to safely join in. There were a few other play areas set up to foster imaginative play: a doll in a cradle and handmade stuffed animals set up in real tree branches and logs that looked like a forest.

Eliza jumped right in. There were no directions or instructions. The children simply played while the teachers worked quietly. The parents were directed to sit along the wall of the room. Baskets of knitting needles and balls of yarn were provided for parents to knit and engage in work like the teachers. This way, they did not interfere in the play but were nearby for the children to see and feel safe.

In my mind, it was genius! My child's first introduction to school was a place to play and imagine. I had been to baby gyms where the parents would have to make the child do tasks, often against their will, lifting them here and directing them there, resulting in tantrums and meltdowns. I had also been over to friends' houses for chaotic playdates in which the well-meaning host parent would pull out so many different toys it became too overwhelming for the children to engage in meaningful or imaginative play.

The Steiner School was so different. First of all, it was calm and quiet, and they allowed the children to do what they do best: explore and play. There were no rules, and nothing was off limits. If two children wanted the same toy, the teacher would calmly introduce a second toy and redirect one of the children to play someplace else.

I picked up a ball of yarn and noticed that the needles already had stitches started on them. To my surprise, my hands went right to work. I remembered how to knit—even though I hadn't knitted a stitch in many years. When I was in third grade, I learned to knit from my elderly babysitter, Sally, who despite her age, was spirited and old school. Sally had always started my projects, but then I could knit rows, and she would finish them. Like riding a bike, I started knitting and felt accomplished to see that I still knew how. I became peacefully engaged in my knitting. It felt very satisfying. For the first time in a while, I was experiencing life in the present moment. As I sat knitting against the wall, I watched my beautiful child play and was amused by the fact that I was probably feeling the same way she was.

Eventually, the children began to get restless, so the teachers would sing a song to guide the transition to what was next. It was time for children—along with the parents, guided by the teachers—to form a circle and sing "Ring Around the Rosie" and other songs with movements. The teachers sang the songs and performed the movements. We watched and followed and joined in without any elaborate instructions. Another song guided the transition to wash our hands.

The class ended with a simple meal of eating oatmeal and drinking tea. It was so civilized and beautiful to sit together at the table: parents, children, and teachers. I wanted to talk to the teachers and ask questions, but then I realized their strong and deliberate silence was setting the example for how to conduct oneself in the classroom and at the table. There were simple phrases, consisting of a few words here and there when necessary, to help guide the children's behavior. If a child acted up, the teachers would address it by firmly but kindly directing them back to the task. Words were offered in a way to teach a growing child rather than to scold. The children in the class were between two and three. It seemed so appropriate for their age and met them where they were. They weren't forced to share, or told what to do. I could feel the compassion and acceptance. It wasn't a free-for-all, and the teachers were in complete control of the classroom. To the core of my being, I could feel this was the kind of education I wanted to provide for my children. I looked forward to the next class.

Ken and I had discussed our future plans for our family, including where we should live. By that point, I had lived in New York City for almost seven years and seen many single friends get married, have children, and then move out of the city. I always thought that wouldn't be me. I saw people raising their kids in New York City and thought it would be a marvelous experience to grow up in one of the most exciting cities in the world.

On the weeks Ken had off, we started to spend more time out of the city, especially at my mother-in-law's house in Hampton Bays. My parents also had a second country home near the Delaware Water Gap, and we would go there and notice how it felt to be outside in nature with the children.

On the weeks Ken would work, I would rotate between every

playground, library, and child destination in a ten-block radius. It was all I could manage with a baby in a baby carrier and a two-year-old in a stroller. I couldn't carry the stroller down the subway steps with a baby carrier, especially during rush hour with commuters whizzing by. Occasionally the three of us would brave the bus or take a cab, but it was difficult and soon enough someone was tired or hungry, or it would rain. It wasn't long before I began to feel trapped in our small apartment, in our small neighborhood, in this big city.

When Ken was off, he would borrow his mother's car and we would leave the city. We felt free. The kids could fall asleep without hassle, and we could park the car and transport groceries and baby gear with a sense of ease. We often drove to Hampton Bays, on the east end of Long Island. I loved bringing my kids to the beach, and before long, we decided to move there. Living in Hampton Bays also meant I could stay home with my children. If we had stayed in New York, I would have returned to work, which had been the plan, but now I felt invested in my new career caring for the children. At times, I found it exhausting and extremely frustrating, but I also found it extremely rewarding and meaningful. Ken found a job at a hospital near Hampton Bays, and we found a vacant lot and planned on building a modular home on it. All of it was exciting and scary. As we were transitioning out of New York, and finishing up the fall term of the parent-child class at the Rudolf Steiner School, I was sad to think that type of education would no longer be available to us.

My search of Waldorf schools on Long Island had revealed a wonderful school in Garden City, but it was an hour and a half from our prospective new location. On the last day of class in the city, I expressed this regret to a fellow mother and was shocked when she told me there was a small early childhood Waldorf program in Sag Harbor, a little more than eighteen miles away from where we would be living. I jumped with excitement, got the name and contact information, and immediately emailed the school. After we moved out there, I visited it and experienced the same simple, warm environment. The school was in the basement of a church that was connected to a beautiful backyard with a garden and chickens! I was moving out of urban Manhattan to have my child run around with chickens behind a church. I was sold instantly, and a few months later, it even inspired us to raise chickens of our own.

Moving with a two-and-a-half-year-old and five-month-old was brutal. I remember literally crying when the movers showed up on New Year's Eve of 2013 as I sat in a sea of boxes. The baby was also crying and there were small unpacked items everywhere and large furniture that was too big to get out of doorways or up the stairs. I again felt helpless and had no idea how to pack everything up. Somehow, we got through it—thanks to the help of a good moving company. After hours and hours of loading and disassembling IKEA furniture, Ken was in the truck with the movers and on his way to Hampton Bays. Eliza was already out there with her grandmother, and my nursing baby and I were driving behind the moving truck. We were closing a chapter in our lives as we left Manhattan, and a new life was ahead of us.

Being a highly sensitive person, change is always challenging for me. Despite the fact I can be impulsive at times, I more often put a lot of thought into my decisions. This was especially true for this move. The universe seemed to support the decision at every step along the way: Ken finding a job, us buying the first lot we saw, and easily connecting with a modular builder. Even though my mind was filled with doubts, I knew this was the right decision. My in-laws graciously allowed us to stay in their summer home while ours was in the building process a mile away.

We were living in a house I was so familiar with. I had spent many summers and fall weekends there, but this was the first time I had been there in the winter. The first couple of weeks, while Ken was at work and it was just my two girls and me, the house seemed so big and empty. In the summertime, it was filled with life and people. The summer days were long, and the January days were short and dark. Manhattan nights would always have some artificial urban streetlight, but out in the more rural setting of Hampton Bays, the nights were dark. My husband and I had lived in apartments in Manhattan, Jersey City, Hoboken, and San Francisco, and spent our college years in Virginia and South Carolina. We hadn't lived in a house since high school, and we were strangers to living in a home. Building a home was also a new experience. Thankfully, my dad was great in advising us along the way.

Ken was busy transitioning into his new job, working twelve hours a day, seven days on seven days off. As a result, a lot of the responsibility for the new house fell to me. Between naps and frequent visits to the library,

I would be on the phone with surveyors, go to the Southampton Building Department, and meet with various subcontractors at our vacant lot with my children in tow.

To say the least, it was a very educational process. We had never owned a home, much less built one. I am grateful to my parents for helping us buy the vacant lot, and we took out a builder's loan that converted into a mortgage. It was all new to me, and I was amazed by the way things were working out. A year prior, we were paying rent and had minimal savings, and the next thing we knew, we were at the closing of the property and making flooring decisions. I had never even thought any of this was possible. We had good jobs, but we also had lots of student loans. Our high Manhattan rent hadn't allowed us to save much, but when you open yourself to new possibilities, factors and forces beyond your control can come into play and make your dreams a reality.

The housing project was moving slowly, and our first winter in Hampton Bays came with lots of snow. There is an image in my mind of the children and me writing "2014" in the deep snow on the deck where we had spent many summer evenings after a long day at the beach. It was my first time seeing snow in this yard and the first time sleeping in the cold ranch-style house that was usually closed down for the winter. However, it had many comforts I did not have living in the city: a washer and dryer that were perfect for drying wet snow pants after playing outside; a big kitchen with counter space that was perfect for making soup and organic homemade baby food; and a driveway that was right next to the house, so if a child fell asleep on an outing to the grocery store the nap could continue while I unloaded the car and tended to the other child.

The house was on a shared lot set far back from the main road. Having only been used in the spring, summer, and fall no one ever had to consider snow shoveling and driveway clearing. After heavy snowfalls, we were often snowed in. Thankfully, one of the year-round neighbors had a friend who had a 4x4 with a plow that cleared a good portion of the icy driveway. However, it was still difficult to pull the car out. On one of our first days, we were running late for our new school. As I was rushing out of the house with children fussing, I got our red Toyota Highlander stuck in a snowbank. We all melted down as we were finding our way in our new life.

It was a thirty-minute drive in the winter, and anywhere up to sixty minutes once spring building and weekenders returned, to get to Our Sons and Daughters, our new early childhood Waldorf School. I felt this school had magically appeared right when I needed it. In the car it was hard occupying a two-and-a-half-year-old and a six-month-old who had to come along for the ride, but I was so comforted by our new school's familiar warmth and simplicity the drive was worth it. To pass the time in the car we would sing songs and eat snacks.

As they got older, we would listen to endless hours of Laura Ingalls Wilder's *Little House on the Prairie* audiobooks. Those simple stories soothed us and helped us survive the many hours of commuting. In New York City, I would have been on a crowded bus with two kids in potential rain and snow, having to carry all the necessary gear on my back and fold up a stroller while wearing a baby carrier and swiping my MetroCard quickly with people behind me rolling their eyes and breathing down my neck. A car with air-conditioning and heat, storage for groceries, and a change of clothes was a gift that kept on giving.

I tried to remind myself of that when I was sitting in stopped traffic with work trucks of every trade coming from western Long Island to service their customers' summer homes. In an effort to cut down on commuting time, Maddy and I would stay in Sag Harbor to eliminate trips back and forth. Since it was my first time dropping off Eliza, it was comforting to stay close to the school.

It was hard to leave my two-and-a half-year-old. There had been so many changes. We would show up to school, usually late and frazzled. I would start to feel calmer as I entered the schoolyard. The teachers working in the yard would greet us warmly. They would sing a song to guide the children to line up for their morning walk around the woods, which inspired me to start looking at the pace I was going. Juggling two kids, moving, and building a house had been a lot, but as I started to read the handouts provided to the parents, and read recommended books on Waldorf education, I began to get a lot out of the school.

I started to learn more about the Austrian philosopher Rudolf Steiner. In the early twentieth century, Steiner founded an esoteric spiritual movement and established biodynamic farming, Waldorf Education, and anthroposophy, which is "the wisdom of the human being." Steiner was a visionary and was described by many as ahead of his time. His direct teachings are a bit hard to understand, but there are many great books by Waldorf educators that put his work into more practical terms.

One of my favorite book recommendations, Sharifa Oppenheimer's *Heaven on Earth*, has a chapter called "Creating Your Family Culture." This chapter made me realize that all the tedious decision-making I was engaged in all day—deciphering how to get organic local food into our home, decisions on discipline, the rhythms of daily routines—weren't the cliché concerns of a housewife but rather the meaningful work of building the foundation of one's life. As the years have gone on, all of this work and research has reaped profound benefits for our family. As spring came, the ground thawed enough for construction to resume; we were also pouring the literal foundation of our life.

As I was caught up nursing, cooking, and changing diapers, I was also mindfully making decisions about the kinds of toys I wanted in our home, as well as limiting screen time, and ensuring plenty of outside time. As a sleep-deprived mom with a history of reluctance in speaking up, it was hard making decisions that go against the norm. Should I politely decline loud light-up toys that I felt were overstimulating? Years later, I realized I was getting overstimulated, along with the children.

People would question my decisions, and I would feel defensive and the need to justify my new forming beliefs. I didn't want to appear pretentious or like a better parent than anyone else, but I was following my heart on the type of parenting that felt right for me. As much as I hated to admit it, I realized I cared about how people thought of me. This type of parenting was unconventional and often deviated from the norm, and it was hard going against the grain. It felt awkward and offensive to ask people to turn off their televisions so my children didn't stop engaging in exploring their three-dimensional, sensory-rich environment to stare at a two-dimensional artificial device that lured them in with flashing lights. I wanted approval or, at the very least, acceptance—a tall order.

I learned so much from watching the teachers at the school. They squatted down and talked to the children at eye level, they listened and smiled and nodded to the children, and they did not always feel the need to say something to fill the space. They worked in the schoolyard, raked leaves outside, and swept the floors while humming in a slow methodical way, not stressfully or anxiously.

*Simplicity Parenting* by Kim John Payne says, "To appreciate the ordinary is an extraordinary gift." I was realizing being a good parent didn't necessarily mean dragging my children to endless music or gymnastic classes and playdates or giving in to excessive amounts of sugar that were present at every turn. In Payne's book, the educator/researcher/counselor talks about simplifying the child's environment, creating rhythm, decreasing scheduling, and filtering out the adult world. The book, and Payne's work, have led to a worldwide parenting community with the aim of overcoming what Payne calls "the undeclared war on childhood." By simplifying, I was noticing how my children and I were thriving. Less external noise could allow us to develop our inner selves. In hindsight, I now realize how much I was raising myself as well as my children.

Part of every Waldorf early childhood school day is devoted to creative expression. An activity would be mindfully and simply set up and strategically placed at a time of the day when the children could properly attend to it. For example, after playing outside, the children would be better able to settle down and engage in a quieter activity. It would vary from drawing with beeswax crayons (which were neatly arranged in a row on a large seashell), to watercolor painting (the primary colors would be set up, and the teacher would paint along with the children as she told a story), as well as beeswax molding, and handwork like sewing, finger crocheting, and knitting.

I was always so moved by the intention and love of these sessions, and I wanted to bring these concepts home. While reading a chapter on developing your child's artistic ability in *You Are your Child's First Teacher,* by Rahima Baldwin, I came across a section called "Freeing Your Own Inner Artist." It recommended doing these artistic activities with your child. Children learn through imitation. The author states that participating alongside your child can help you reclaim and nourish your own inner innate creative ability, which was probably squelched through lack of use or beliefs such as "I'm not good enough" or "I can't paint."

The light bulb flashed over my head. I definitely owned a lot of these limiting beliefs. While I was reading the book, I was also seeing a new therapist who was helping me do a lot of inner child healing. The time, energy, intention, and love I put into caring for my children was also healing me. One of the many reasons I feel so passionately about Waldorf education is that it isn't a spectator sport. The teachers live the work, the teachings come from the heart and love inside them, and you can feel it. It's not just dogmatic and arbitrary knowledge that they learned and recite to the students. The learning happens on a deeper level because of the way it is lived through the teachers.

In the "Freeing Your Own Inner Artist" section, Baldwin references *The Artist's Way* by Julia Cameron. In an aha moment, I figured I should read Cameron's book. I'm glad I did. It inspired me to take the book's recommended twelve-week self-study course of creative recovery which, in turn, led me to write this book. I had never thought of myself as a creative person but through watching my children, who were deeply connected with their creativity, I slowly started to connect with my own inner artist. Watching my children create helped me to realize it is an innate ability. The meaningful work of becoming a mother and paving a creative path for my children has helped me to experience the healing and growth, which has allowed my own creative sparks.

One morning a week, the school would hold a craft circle for parents in the upstairs of the church. The parents would make homemade crafts for the schools' seasonal festivals. In the fall, we would make lanterns out of recycled glass jars with beautifully colored tissue paper glued onto them for the lantern walk. The lanterns would be carried by the children and family participants to light their way during the October evening while walking through the woods and singing songs. This would occur after listening to a story told by the teacher outside around the fire. A simple meal of cider and soup would be served. In a beautiful way, this simple festival demonstrates to the children, and their families, how the days get shorter in the fall.

In December, we would make candles from beeswax to use during the Spiral of Lights, the winter festival. During the Spiral of Lights, each child holds a real candle in a real apple candleholder decorated with a small sprig of evergreen. With the other hand each child would hold the teacher or parent's hand and in their turn would walk around a giant spiral made of evergreen branches which had been delicately arranged on the floor. The room would be dark—except for the candles—and silent, with the exception of a song sung for each child by all the family and friends sitting outside the giant spiral, along the edge of the room. My eyes would fill with tears as I watched each of my children holding their candle with reverence and gently placing it next to a seashell that was strategically placed along the spiral. When the ceremony was over, the whole spiral was lit with the beautiful apple candles as we honored the light within each child.

In the spring, our craft circle would make a variety of crafts for the May Fair—a fun outdoor celebration in which the children danced around the maypole holding brightly colored ribbons. They would also make flower crowns and fairy capes, dig for crystals, and more. A teacher would dress up as 'the Pocket Fairy', and she he would walk around the fair handing out handmade gnomes, birds and other special treats, which had been made by the parents.

These craft circles were intimidating to me at first. The other parents and atmosphere were very welcoming, but I was skeptical I wouldn't be able to make any of these beautiful crafts. Besides my very basic knit stitch, I had little handwork experience and felt my creative insecurity. After a few weeks, I learned it only took a little practice, patience, and confidence in myself. It was liberating, satisfying, and empowering to be able to make a beautiful craft for a child with my own two hands.

Before I knew it, I was buying my own supplies and sewing felt sheets to make small stuffed fish and mice at home in front of my children who thought of me as a master crafter. You can probably find images on Pinterest of way more elaborate and better-crafted items, but that isn't the point. When you make something like that by hand, you can feel the time and effort someone has put into it. Despite its novice flaws, the sheer conviction in the attempt and intention to make something from the heart is what art is. Unraveling my creative insecurities was wonderful and therapeutic.

When new parents would join the school and come to the circle with the same intimidation and comments that they weren't crafty, I would smile and say, "Hey, if I can do it, so can you." I contemplated these lessons during the many hours I spent making these items. When the sun was shining on the schoolyard on a bright May day with flowers blooming, those handmade items that members of the community spent all winter making were the perfect touch for a truly beautiful celebration of the glory of spring.

I felt I had come full circle. I started off intimidated but then—guided by the teachers at the school—went on to co-lead the group with a very creative and knowledgeable friend. I enjoyed the wonderful time connecting to the like-minded parents the school attracted.

During the craft circles and in the school parking lot after drop-off, I was getting to know these very down-to-earth parents. Often the question would come up of what I did for work. It was an uncomfortable question for me. My former days of being a physical therapist in New York City seemed like a lifetime ago, but the image of a rural stay-at-home mom leading a craft circle didn't feel like an accurate description either. I was grateful to be so intertwined in my kids' lives, but I had never planned to stay at home. I had thought of it as a temporary circumstance while we were in transition.

I had moved to New York City to pave my own path and rebel against the traditional suburban life that felt forced on me growing up. In those earlier days, I had not anticipated the profound maternal shift and development of a mother's intuition. As I experienced this intuition—as it related to the needs of my children—I became more deeply connected to who I was. Living in a rural/suburban town two hours from my former urban home and driving thirty minutes to school, somewhere along the way I had lost the connection to that New York City girl I had been. But to my pleasant surprise, my organic connection to my children and to motherhood turned out to be exactly what I was seeking and had been longing for.

Several months later, when our new house was finished, we moved in. Despite all the changes, and the long transitioning process, I truly felt at home. I was gratefully living in the present moment in this new life. Waldorf education guided the way. I felt deeply connected to what I was doing, and I also felt the seeds of bigger things to come. Life was unfolding before my eyes, and for now that was enough.

# CHAPTER 3

# Spring Awakening: The (Relatively) Fast Track of Transformation

The east end of Long Island brings summer waves of vacationing weekenders getting away from the city to the promised land of luxurious summer euphoria. As young professionals in our pre-parent days, Ken and I would wait in Penn Station in front of the electronic board that identified the track numbers of the trains. When our train was announced, we would run like lemmings, along with the huge crowd of others, to board the train. As the train headed for Jamaica Station, it was often standing room only. At Jamaica, we transferred across the platform to the Montauk train, which stopped in various towns on the south fork collectively known as the Hamptons. During the two-hour train ride, the crowd would decrease slightly at each stop. Twenty or so stops later, by the time Hampton Bays was announced, the calmer scene on the train would contain a lot fewer passengers and have released most of the city chaos.

The stress from city living would unravel further as we arrived in the charming hamlet of Hampton Bays. We would then head toward the Ponquogue Bridge. As we approached the fifty-five-foot apex of the half-mile bridge and crossed over the Shinnecock Bay, the weightlessness would evolve into a feeling of floating. Seeing the natural beach landscape—the bay, the barrier island, and the ocean beach—I would feel the struggle of life in New York City falling away and feel at ease. On the other side of the bridge, we would make a left and drive to the end of the road where the bay and ocean meet at the inlet. I would get out of the car, stand on the rock jetty, and put my arms out to receive the natural energy that felt so powerful there.

As I shifted from a Hamptons weekender to year-round resident, I got to really experience firsthand the metamorphosis these tiny hamlets go through. I watched as the crazy summers gave way to smaller crowds, epic falls, and Indian summers. They say September in the Hamptons is the best-kept secret, and I agree. On the other hand, the glorious falls give way to the dreaded winters everyone had warned me about. "Don't move out there. The winters are a nightmare!" This was in reference to the vacant ghost town feeling after Labor Day. The locals even call the Tuesday after Labor Day "Tumbleweed Tuesday."

All in all, it was a relatively graceful transition from Manhattan life to life on the East End. Now that I was living there full time, it felt as if I had responded to an inner calling from this glorious natural environment. I had always felt a therapeutic restoration when I entered into nature, especially around the element of water. Years later, learning more about the native Shinnecock Indians who inhabited much of this land before it was taken from them by European settlers, I could see and feel the sacred magic that reverberated here. And I understood why it was called 'good ground.'

Living in New York City taught me a lot. I still go back there regularly to visit friends and go to events. I also go when I am feeling a need to be challenged, inspired, or pushed outside my comfort zone in a way only New York City can. Living in the Hamptons is just the opposite. The natural wonderland provides a soothing environment for my children and me.

People often remarked how hard it must have been to adjust from life in a big city like New York, where more than 1.6 million live in Manhattan alone, to a town with a little more than thirteen thousand people. They seemed surprised when I told them how much I loved it here. Even though I was still quite busy running after two kids, I felt more at peace than ever. There was a sense of ease running an errand in town in under ten minutes and a beautiful simplicity in having one health food store and two yoga studios as compared to the many in New York. I quickly started recognizing familiar faces at places I frequented, and I even started making connections between Hampton Bays and the town of Sag Harbor, where I drove the kids to school every day. I liked being with my children in the small town, holding their hands and walking down Main Street. Compared to the big city, or the congested suburbs, it was a place we could all grasp.

As the season changed in the Hamptons, I continued to study Rudolf Steiner's work in Waldorf education, and it resonated deeply, personally and as a parent. As I dropped my children off at school every day, I noticed an intentionally repeating day-to-day rhythm that helped the children understand what to expect. The weekly rhythms were consistent as well, and they would slowly change in accordance with the seasons.

As my connection to myself grew deeper, facilitated by my new natural surroundings, I loved that my children were going to a school that supported them. The stories told by the teachers of squirrels collecting nuts in the fall would shift to the root children sleeping underground in the winter, and then crocuses waking up in the spring. The way the children (and teachers) would rake the leaves in the fall, sleigh ride in the winter, and work in the garden in the spring was a meaningful way to learn and celebrate the diversity of seasons we experience in the Northeast.

As fate would have it, we ended up moving to Hampton Bays on January 1, 2014, in the middle of a very hard winter. I would send Eliza to her new school in her 2T snow pants, and the school day would begin with outdoor play regardless of the weather. I remember the steep hill in the schoolyard that led up to the fenced-in section where the animals lived. She struggled to get up in her heavy snow boots and bulky snow pants.

It was hard to watch my poor little two-year-old get frustrated and upset trying to negotiate the steep icy hill in her winter gear. It even led me to initially question having young children be outdoors in such weather conditions. The teacher calmly and confidently told me a child learns it is winter when they put on snow pants and struggle up a snowy hill with a cold wind on their face. This learning through experience seemed more significant than looking and learning about a calendar. It was so profound experiencing the learning alongside my children. The teacher would hold the hand of a struggling child, but not eliminate the obstacle altogether, as I wanted to do.

By the next winter, we moved one last time from my mother-in-law's house in Hampton Bays and into our new home. It was a dream come true. We had a driveway and counter space—something New Yorkers seriously appreciate. We had room for all of our things and then some! We had a fenced-in backyard for the children (and the chickens) and a swing set. If I needed to run inside for a moment and grab a hat, my children could be outside and even alone for quick moments. In New York, leaving children on the street was obviously not an option and required two locked doors and stairs to tackle again if I forgot something. It was those simple things that made life so good.

That December, while visiting my parents in New Jersey for the holidays, I took a yoga class with a teacher whose class I always loved going to when I was passing through town. As usually happened, her enlightened talk at the beginning of class inspired me. She talked about the days getting shorter and the winter approaching. The moving inward, and the darkness of the shortened days, was an opportunity for self-reflection. A light sparked. My basic needs were being better met in my new house. My children were now one and a half and three and a half. It was still hard, but I felt I was beginning to shift out of survival mode. I felt I now had the luxury to continue my inward journey. I picked up where I had left off, contemplating life's meaning.

I was so happy, yet some of the old discomforts resurfaced. During the previous four years, I had been too consumed with motherhood to even contemplate such questions. Now that I had a little bit more sleep, my mind started to fill up with what kind of life I wanted to live and create, what my calling was, and what kind of mother and wife I wanted to be.

A friend of mine had recently taken a five-day workshop called "The Basic Training." The contents of the course were purposely not revealed, making it a bit hard to describe. The company offers a free trial workshop to introduce some of the self-growth exercises participants will undergo during the training. One sample exercise involved identifying a goal, a wish, or lifelong dream and imagining it without limitations, then sharing it with a partner. Most of the trial participants were friends and family members of people who had been referred by people who had already taken the full five-day workshop.

I liked the free sample, but I was reluctant to sign up for the full course. There were the obvious superficial/logistical excuses: arranging childcare, the expense, and living two hours away. I felt an uncomfortable feeling in my stomach. It was a familiar feeling. I felt these superficial reasons were legitimate. I wasn't a recent college graduate looking to find myself; I was a full-time married mother of two young children. There was school transportation, bedtime routines, and meal preparation to consider. Plus, as a mother, I was reluctant to farm out the work of being a mom, but then I remembered *life begins outside your comfort zone.*

While my friend was encouraging me to take the course, I became defensive. As I heard myself justifying these logistical situations, I realized there were deeper fears I was also facing: fear of the unknown, fear of the consequences of following my heart, fear of being selfish, fear of being a bad wife and mother, fear of failure, and fear of facing the skeletons in my closet.

Despite my fears, excuses, and initial resistance, my curiosity and interest in personal growth won out. I enrolled in the course. Now I needed to make arrangements to attend the course. It has always been hard for me to admit I need help, much less accept it. My head was spinning. Yet, things fell into place. I had stopped breastfeeding Maddy a few months prior, so I was no longer needed for nighttime feedings. I pushed through my resistance and accepted help.

I arrived in New York City on Wednesday afternoon. I walked into the conference room and was greeted by friendly staff members and twenty or so other participants. They mostly lived in New York City and in the tri-state area. They represented a wide range of ages, professions, and backgrounds. Most participants had been referred by friends and family. We were all unsure about what to expect. The course started at 5pm and went until almost midnight. It was the same schedule on Thursday and Friday.

Saturday's session lasted all day, and by Sunday the unfamiliar faces felt like fellow soldiers, connected and linked by the camaraderie of going through an intense battle of transformation. We listened to lectures, worked in small groups, and participated in exercises and visualizations, all designed to facilitate self-growth. The biggest breakthrough for me was recognizing old patterns and beliefs about myself. It brought healing and helped clear away any pain from the past that I was holding onto, so the present and future could be whatever I wanted to make them. It was a cathartic process, and not always easy, but as promised, we experienced self-growth and breakthroughs. This occurred in March 2015 after my winter inward reflection, and it was a true spring awakening!

Having released the anchor of being a victim to circumstance, and letting go of my excuses for not creating a future filled with the things I desired, I came home energized and ready to embark on new adventures that had previously scared me. The course warns that you are now wide-open, in a good way, and yet cautions you that you are now more vulnerable as well.

It is recommended that you complete the two follow-up courses in the three-part series. I felt torn. On the one hand, I loved the transformative experience and was eager for more. On the other hand, I felt I had invested enough time, energy, and money (for now). I also knew that I was a seeker, and this was only the start of a long series of opportunities for growth that I believed were going to occur. I felt a bit uncomfortable declining the next class, but I did.

Prior to taking the course, it is requested you fill out a questionnaire. One question asks you to list areas in your life that you want to improve. I had listed two. The first being my interest in opening a small business from home. Several months back, I had connected with a friend of my parents who had a breast pump rental service in New Jersey and was interested in expanding his business to Long Island. Since giving birth, I had become very passionate about breastfeeding. I had breastfed my older daughter for eighteen months and my younger one for fourteen months. Even though I was no longer breastfeeding, I felt very connected to mothers who had recently given birth and were breastfeeding and needed support. Since I had a lot of personal experience with breastfeeding and using a breast pump, it was a natural segue to starting my own local branch of my friend's breast pump rental service.

I was interested in pursuing this, partly because I didn't feel it was time yet to return to physical therapy. My children were young, so it made sense for me to work with breastfeeding mothers as a vendor—and not as a health care professional—which felt like a lighter responsibility. I hadn't pursued the business prior to the course. Because I was moving and being a full-time mom, I didn't feel I had the time and the energy to start a business. Once I had taken the course, I was more motivated and confident. I was ready to forge ahead and confront my fear of failure, which was also a major deterrent for starting the business. *What if I put myself out there and failed? They say most small businesses fail in the first year. Why would mine be any different?*

The excess mind chatter in my head that I had struggled with for so long was often fear based. Looking back on events in my life, I noticed how paralyzing fear could be. Moving to California and breaking up with Ken was an example. I pushed past those fears, but they stayed with me and haunted me. The course helped me face my fears which in turn liberated me. I had realized my fears were not me, and so the fears lost their power over me. Moving on felt almost easy compared to the fear itself. Of course, the awareness and getting there can be tricky.

There were some small costs with starting the business, so failing would also mean losing money. Nevertheless, I went ahead and pushed through my fear of failing. I called my business Breast Is Best. I loved the freedom of working for myself. It was fun, creative, and exhilarating. As it turned out, two years later, I did decide to close down Breast Is Best. Did I fail? Maybe. Some would say yes, but to me, it didn't feel like a failure at all. It was a wonderful exercise in changing my beliefs and facing my fears. Although my business didn't succeed, I learned a lot and that knowledge was invaluable to me in later endeavors.

The second area of my life I wanted to improve was my body image. For as long as I could remember, I had struggled with my weight. I longed to be thinner, but it felt shallow to be consumed with this thought. As a mother, and an experienced adult, I knew there were so many other deeper problems I could be facing. However, I also realized it wasn't about vanity but rather a longing for health and beauty both inside and out.

Again, the course assisted me in gaining determination and strength in addressing the old limiting belief that losing weight was hard for me. This belief had been built on previous experiences that had occurred over and over since I was a child. I was a healthy-sized baby and toddler, but as an adolescent, I always had a shorter and rounder figure rather than the taller, thinner one I would have preferred. It is all relative, but I would frequently compare my body to others, and I felt tremendously insecure about it. I remember being consoled by people who loved me. I was told that I was "larger boned" and "still growing." I was told not to worry about my weight.

However, years later, I would have flashbacks of painful times trying on clothes that were tighter and higher in size than I thought was acceptable. I dreaded bathing suit shopping and remember being encouraged by my mom to wear one-piece bathing suits to conceal my round belly—even though I wanted to wear a two-piece suit. I vividly remember hating yearly physical exams at my pediatrician's office. Being weighed and where I ranked on the BMI charts filled me with shame. I wasn't morbidly obese, and am not sure what constitutes the dreaded three letter f-word that I refuse to say in front of my daughters to this day.

So, yes, there was evidence to support my belief that losing weight was a struggle. The cycle would continue in high school, college, and into my twenties as my weight would yo-yo up and down with various dieting efforts. Taking the workshop/training helped me clearly identify what I wanted—to lose weight and have a healthy, attractive body—and identify the obstacles to getting it. Thanks to the course, I was able to let go of my long-held belief that it was hard for me to lose weight and to reject the idea that I am genetically predisposed not to be thin. I faced the shame of my failed past attempts. I acknowledged how grateful I was for my health and how well my body had served me throughout the years—even though it wasn't always at the weight I would have desired. At that point, I had given birth twice and hadn't made any solid attempts to lose weight in years. Now I was ready to get to work, but how?

Once I acknowledged and cleared away those vulnerable, painful, and ultimately nonproductive feelings, I had a breakthrough. To see if I had ever been successful, I reflected on the many times I tried to lose weight. It turns out, I had had some transient success in the past when I was accountable weekly and set small realistic goals with Weight Watchers. Those past attempts didn't last, because I would stop going. It takes courage and humility to walk into a Weight Watchers meeting, especially when they ask if you have tried the program before—and you shamefully say yes.

This time was different. I marched right in, already feeling empowered. I faced my fear and acknowledged that I like who I am. I wanted to lose weight. I looked right in the eye of the employee at the desk and said, "I am here to lose weight, and I plan on being successful." I joined and lost thirty-five pounds over the next two years and am still maintaining it today.

To be sure, there were ups and downs. Even after I was down ten, fifteen or twenty pounds, I was surprised—despite all the successes—that it was still possible to feel shame after having a bad day of eating poorly. I fought through it and stayed focused on the fact that I was consistently losing weight. It was a powerful lesson of loving yourself where you are. I thought many times about how I would like myself so much more if I was twenty pounds lighter. I would get there and still be face-to-face with the shame. My thoughts were the problem—not the twenty pounds.

I eventually made it to my goal. I felt euphoric celebrating my thirty-five-pound loss. The woman who checked me in that first day said she knew I was going to be successful by the way I walked in. It took a lot of hard work: daily monitoring my food intake, facing the scale every week, the ups and downs, and being committed to the long term. I am still doing the work, and I still experience setbacks. However, making up my mind that I can do it and letting go of my former limiting beliefs worked then and still guides me now.

Improving these areas of my life, proved to me how much taking the training had been worth it. On the surface, nothing in life had changed. Yet, I felt like I had a new lease on life. This momentum continued, and a few months later a dear friend turned me on to the 2015 Hay House Summit. This was a free collection of audio lessons, videos, and movies from more than one hundred of the world's leading experts in the field of self-help and wellness. It was the next step in my New Age education.

I started listening to the summit's founder, Louise Hay, and her work on self-love and positive affirmations. Most of my reading in the past few years had been less about my own self-growth and more about parenting. Through the therapy I had done with Ruth a few years ago, and more recently with the course, I understood the negative self-talk in my head was unproductive and not who I was. However, I hadn't realized I could replace those voices in my head with something more positive and productive. Louise Hay, an American motivational author of many self-help books, is best known for *You Can Heal Your Life,* which she wrote at age sixty after recovering from cervical cancer. I watched her videos and listened to her talks. Her radiant self and soothing voice uplifted me. Her positive affirmations were the perfect example of the thoughts I wanted to think.

Hay was also the founder of Hay House, a publishing company of books and audiobooks by more than 130 authors. Hay's work led to my discovery of Esther Hicks and her work on The Law of Attraction. As I continued listening to the summit, I was exposed to many other great authors, including Wayne Dyer.

The inspiration from these wonderful authors (Hay, Hicks, and Dyer), the training, and the weekly support meetings at Weight Watchers all started to come together. I listened to YouTube recordings of Louise Hay's power thoughts while I took walks. Declaring that "I live in a loving, abundant, harmonious universe, and I am grateful" was helpful in realizing I am not a victim. I truly was happy, but I needed to get into a regular practice of affirming it.

Listening to Esther Hicks channeling the teachings of Abraham and The Law of Attraction helped me in creating my own reality, and I began to feel so much better. My life started to improve. The Law of Attraction is the belief that positive or negative thoughts bring positive or negative experiences into a person's life. As I practiced and affirmed positive thoughts, more positive experiences would come. It was simple, but powerful.

Our society wants instant gratification, and as much as it was working for me, it was a slow process. I could connect to the power of the positive feelings right away, but the manifestations took time. That was okay, because I was slowly starting to see and feel the results. Going about my daily errands and caring for the kids felt lighter and easier. I would feel grateful for the grocery store having the items I wanted, getting a good parking space or bumping into a loving friend. On the drive home, I was thankful for the beautiful beach town I lived in and the beautiful home that accommodated us in so many wonderful ways.

As I pulled into my driveway, I would feel gratitude seeing our chickens that laid us delicious fresh eggs, and even more gratitude for my beautiful daughters who would jump out of the car to excitedly pick up the chickens. The girls were thriving before my eyes. I also loved and felt grateful for my husband, Ken. He loved and supported me mentally, physically, and financially. As I affirmed what I had and truly connected with those feelings, I felt that I could go on and on.

Of course, there were days then—and still now—when I didn't feel like dancing and relishing in all I have. The difference is, I don't give it as much power as I used to. Previously, on those darker days, I would easily go on a downward spiral of despair and say, "I'm not happy—maybe I need to run away and find happiness somewhere else." Now, I take a bad day or a bad moment and look at it as just that: a bad moment. I notice the momentum and try to get out of the way. I often go to bed earlier on those nights, and as my fatigue increases, I have less strength to handle negative thoughts. I drift off to sleep, and by the next morning, it's hard to imagine the discomfort from the day before even existed. I feel refreshed, renewed, and ready to start a new day with fresh momentum in a positive direction, ready for action on the things that plagued me the day before.

As I was gaining a deeper understanding of the laws of the universe, the momentum continued. I was following this work of positive thinking into the summer, fall and winter. Then in the spring of 2016, one year after the breakthrough training, I took another course with the same motivational speaker and life coach, Liz Wolfe. She hosted a weekend workshop on abundance and prosperity.

The previous year's course had been a five-day class with more than twenty people in a hotel conference room in Midtown Manhattan. This was a two-day weekend class, with a little more than ten participants, in her beautiful two-story brownstone uptown in Hamilton Heights near City College. I loved the more intimate arrangement of this workshop. Since I easily get overstimulated, this was perfect for me.

Liz started her workshop by stating that she had acquired her home with the help of abundant thinking. I reflected back to my wedding and my home, neither of which I thought Ken and I could afford, yet I deeply wanted them. I was extremely grateful when they manifested. Liz referenced many great quotes that I found helpful, including this one: "Are we grateful because we have so much—or do we have so much because we are grateful?"

I felt that being grateful and thinking positively had brought me so much. The two-day workshop was made up of lectures, exercises, guided visualizations, and making vision boards. It was interesting to examine my old patterns and beliefs about money and to realize how they had shaped my life.

When Liz referenced Esther Hicks and Wayne Dyer, it was a beautiful synchronicity. I had been following them on my own. Looking back at my notebook from the course, I came across this quote from Lao Tzu, which sums up the power of positive thoughts:

Watch your thoughts, they become your words.
Watch your words, they become your actions.
Watch your actions, they become your habits.
Watch your habits, they become your character.
Watch your character, it becomes your destiny.

Another concept from the course, attributable to Liz and Esther Hicks alike, talks about manifesting a desired outcome. Esther Hicks' well-known book, *Ask and It Is Given,* suggests we can use the law of attraction to help accomplish our dreams by going through the process of asking, allowing, and receiving. Liz expanded on the work and added giving and gratitude to these steps, because abundance comes from letting go—and scarcity comes from holding on. Wayne Dyer said, "Abundance is not something we acquire. It is something we tune in to."

I loved seeing the way it was all coming together: the work I was following, the exercises, and the discussions in the workshop about thinking abundantly and recognizing old patterns of poverty thinking. Since I was operating a small business, this was all very valuable, but the deeper value was in personal growth and recognizing my beliefs and patterns. I was beginning to make life decisions that were in my highest good and less driven by scarcity thinking.

I reflected back to when I decided to move to San Francisco, and then living in New York City during PT school, when I didn't have a reliable income. Poverty thinking would have discouraged me from the choices that brought so much value into my life. I didn't realize it at the time, but I was actually practicing abundant thinking even then. PT school was an investment in my future, and living in New York City and San Francisco in my twenties wasn't a lavish decision. It was good for my soul. I somehow had faith I would find the financial means to make it all work, and I did. Someone else may make decisions other than the ones I made, but the point is to make decisions from a place of abundant thinking and not just on the practicalities of finances.

They say money can't buy happiness, and it started to occur to me that financial success seemed to be somewhat arbitrary, depending on who you compare yourself to, the personal choices you make on purchases, where you live, and ultimately your state of mind. Therefore, staying connected with your visions and goals should be the guide. Abundant thinking doesn't encourage reckless spending or discourage practical ways to live and save. It requires you don't sell yourself short in order to save a buck. I still pay those student loans every month without regret—and maybe one day they will even get canceled!

As much as income levels changed, my perception hadn't all that much. Yes, there was less money in my bank account when I was in college, but somehow, there always seemed to be enough. Even when Ken and I drove back from San Francisco, when we had both lost our jobs, we camped along the way because we couldn't afford hotel rooms. We saved Subway rewards cards to get free sandwiches, which we ate at every stop. When we look back we laugh, because regardless of the lack of funds, it was a great adventure. We felt free. At the time, I felt like we had it all and were following our dreams, dreams that maybe would pay off and maybe wouldn't. We have great stories from that trip and wouldn't have changed it for the world. I have never classified myself as rich financially, but I would say I have lived a very rich life and am very satisfied and eager for more. Liz's course helped me make sense of all this and was 2016's spring awakening.

Now that I was more clearly focused on what I wanted, more door-opening experiences continued to come my way. I was creating the reality of the life I wanted to live. Spring 2017 brought an incredible opportunity for me to travel to Africa for a yoga retreat. A friend was leading an eight-day expedition to Rwanda and Uganda. When she mentioned it to me, I immediately wanted to go, but then the resistance came. My first thought was how to handle the expense, but then awareness quickly set in. I connected to the gratitude of this wonderful opportunity coming to me, which connected me back to thinking abundantly.

From there, I started thinking about money. We had been advised to save up for a rainy day. It occurred to me, if this wasn't the unexpected opportunity I was saving up for, then what was? This helped me let go of my fear and poverty thinking—as well as some savings!

The next point of resistance was leaving my family. My children were five and three at that point, and as much as I wanted to go to Africa, I feared leaving my family and flying fifteen hours to the other side of the world. Although the trip was only eight days, it was on another continent. It felt exorbitant, and initially, it was hard to give myself permission. Thankfully, Ken, my parents, and my in-laws stepped up to assist with watching the children. I stepped outside my comfort zone and decided to go. I successfully navigated past the resistance and felt grateful that this once-in-a-lifetime experience had come. From the day-to-day work I had been doing and the spring awakenings I had experienced, I truly felt I had helped open the door and assisted in this opportunity coming my way.

Going to Africa was a dream come true. My dormant love of world traveling was reactivated and reconnected me to my time in India. Being a mother now, the India trip felt like it had occurred in a former life. When I was on the playground with my babies, I was glad to daydream back to that wonderful trip—especially when I wasn't feeling the miraculous joys of motherhood and was exhausted running around after a one-year-old and a three-year-old in a breast milk-stained shirt with hair that I hadn't washed for days. I would get insecure hearing other people's inspiring tales out in the world. Of course I was only half listening, because one baby was crying and the other was demanding a snack. I was also thinking of what to make for dinner and if I could fit a trip to the grocery store in before nap time. In times like these, I would thank God I had some former memory of exotic adventures.

Although I was loving being a mother, this trip to Africa helped me reconnect with who I was before motherhood. Experiencing the land of a thousand hills and the transformation Rwanda went through after the 1994 genocide, I felt transformed as well. I remember tagging along and sitting at a dinner meeting at our hotel in Kigali. The meeting was between a successful New York mother and CEO, and a successful mother of three from Ghana who was also a CEO in Africa. As I sat listening with the other powerful women we were traveling with, I was inspired. If these women could do it, why couldn't I? It rekindled the fire inside me that was hungry, but not sure yet for what exactly.

Driving through the countryside, exiting Rwanda and crossing the border into Uganda, seemed to be the right place to start looking. The opportunity to reflect and recharge in a furnished tent on the shores of Lake

Bunyonyi was uplifting. We were staying in a rustic and enchanting eco-resort and retreat center that positively impacts the local rural community. During the last leg of the trip, we took a dusk boat safari and a dawn jeep safari into the Queen Elizabeth National Park in Uganda. We experienced close encounters with lions, hippos, baboons, water buffalo, elephants, warthogs, and more.

The trip was enhanced further with extraordinary daily yoga classes taught by my friend. There were stops at project sites established by the Paper Fig Foundation, a nonprofit organization based in New York. The organization's mission is to use fashion and fine arts to empower economic development in Africa. We had the honor of traveling with the director of the organization. We visited a medical clinic, a sewing school graduation, and the home of a young fashion designer. He was given the opportunity to come to New York on a scholarship established by the foundation. These were soul-warming experiences that came just in time for that year's spring awakening.

I returned home rejuvenated—after I recovered from jet lag. I was ready for what was next. I just wasn't sure what it was. I continued caring for the kids, while also reading, listening, and absorbing work from the Hay House authors. The summer came, and I was offered a physical therapy job at my husband's hospital. Both of my children were going to be in school full-time for the first time in the fall, and this job came at a time when I was available to take it.

I was flattered to be wanted—I hadn't been a full-time professional since before the birth of my children—and I was tempted. The job would be close to home and would be flexible around my kids' school. As I took the time to carefully consider this wonderful opportunity, I started to envision shackles. I was on the cusp of freedom. For six years, I had been caring for my children. As much as the financial income and reentry to my former career was calling me, my inner voice was louder. It was telling me to take some time.

I gratefully declined the position and ended the summer in Ireland on a family vacation. My sister-in-law had invited us to visit her husband's family in Ireland. My in-laws went as well, and we traveled around the country together. It was my second international trip of the year! The Law of Attraction says, "The essence of that which is like unto itself is drawn."

We took a red-eye from New York to Dublin, drove north through Belfast, and stayed in Londonderry for a few days. We explored Northern Ireland and the magnificent Giant's Causeway, which one poll listed as fourth on a list of natural wonders of the world. The giant cliffs that overlook the sea are a place where earth and heaven feel like they are one. It was like the Hampton Bays inlet at home but on a much grander scale.

We then headed south, traveling through the Connemara National Park. We arrived in the beautiful, upbeat harbor town of Galway with its cobblestone walkways and narrow streets. We drove from the west coast straight across the country through the central lowlands back to Dublin on the east coast. The green and serene landscape in Ireland was enchanting. Looking out the window at the hills, as we were traveling around the country, was glorious. The countryside was inspiring, and it was wonderful to be experiencing it with my children. They also fell in love with Ireland. We visited fairy gardens and leprechaun museums. We were pleasantly surprised to find little fairy doors hidden throughout our travels. While at the breathtaking Kylemore Abbey and Victorian Walled Garden—as we admired the incredible architecture—we were delighted to find a small fairy door in a tree outside the café where we had lunch. The land had a magic to it that we could all feel.

We came home, and as the high energy of summer started to wind down into the fall, Eliza was entering first grade and Madeleine prekindergarten. Eliza had aged out of the early childhood Waldorf School we loved in Sag Harbor and entered a new school in Aquebogue. Due to my inability to transport one kid to the north fork and one to the south fork of Long Island, I also enrolled Maddy there. Maddy would be going to school five full days to be on the same schedule as Eliza, and I would now have more freedom with both kids in school from nine until three. It was a big change for all of us.

Their new school was wonderful, but no longer being in a Waldorf school was a big adjustment. It had clearly become a great love of mine. Despite the very warm welcome we had received in the new school, it felt like we had moved again and were starting over. We were saying goodbye to our old community and were now traveling in a new direction.

Fall had come. I was being gentle with myself and giving myself permission to move slowly while digesting all these changes. The changes were hard for me, but the girls quickly made new friends—and their transition was fairly seamless.

Right before we had left for Ireland, I started seeing a new therapist. Although I had declared my happiness and dismissed a lot of my former limiting beliefs, I wanted to continue my journey within. I hadn't been actively looking for a therapist. An accidental yoga studio schedule mix-up started a cosmic treasure hunt. I intended on going to an eight o'clock class but landed instead in a recovery support group meeting. I hadn't realized that support groups met at the studio. During the meeting I met someone who gave me her therapist's card. I was always very open to the benefits of therapy, especially with my previous positive results from working with Ruth in grad school. I called this new therapist, Lois, and started seeing her.

This was a wonderful opportunity to go further within and look at why change was so unnerving for me. Lois helped guide me through this process with a variety of therapeutic approaches, including hypnotherapy. I had heard of hypnosis. Once when I was in my twenties, I had been hypnotized in hopes of it helping me lose weight. That hypnosis had been unsuccessful. My experience with Lois and hypnotherapy was very different. It was more like a deep guided meditation. Unlike the sleepy journey to the unconscious of the last time, I felt very safe and present.

Going to the hypnotherapy sessions, I realized the difficulty with change I was experiencing as a parent at the new school was triggered by painful childhood memories—specifically moving in fourth grade and then changing schools again in fifth grade. In these sessions with Lois, I did a lot of inner child healing work. Previously in the Basic Training workshop, there had been some exercises geared toward healing your inner child. I had also done inner child work while listening to Louise Hay meditations.

Working with Lois, the third time was a charm. Lois's holistic approach included essential oils, Reiki (an energy therapy), psychotherapy, and sessions with family members. It really helped deepen my connection to myself, and I let go of old baggage I didn't even realize I was hanging onto. Unpacking the old baggage and then clearing it away was valuable on my road to self-growth and healing. I was so glad I pursued that cosmic treasure hunt and took the humble leap to go back to therapy. As

I continued to do the work, and connect and listen to my inner voice, amazing things continued to happen. I truly believe if I had taken the PT job, all of this valuable self-discovery—and even this book—would not have happened.

I had developed my own cycle of active Hamptons' summers that led to the calmer, but still glorious, falls. As the days got shorter and darker—which at one time I had mistaken for unhappiness—I now understood these winter days were an opportunity for introspection. Now, with each winter, as Hampton Bays would quiet down, I was afforded the time to slow down and go within. As the renewal of spring came, I had new awakenings that were becoming beautifully layered year after year. It was as if the universe had planned it perfectly. Each year, I was going deeper within and getting stronger. I was ready and eager for more self-growth and expansion.

This year as Spring 2018 approached, things would be different. As the going got tough, I was ready to get going.

# CHAPTER 4

# Clearing Out My Closet

I was now fully engaged in my creative recovery. *The Artist's Way: A Spiritual Guide to High Creativity* by Julia Cameron, which I had fortuitously discovered, had become my guide. Following it diligently, I was writing every morning in what Cameron calls 'morning pages', which helped me go deeper into my creative recovery. Morning pages involves writing three handwritten pages every morning when you first wake up.

I loved my new ritual of doing something for myself first thing in the morning. Before the day got at me, I could more easily connect with my inner voice. Some days, writing three pages would be challenging. I initially didn't feel like I had much to say, but as I patiently persisted, the creativity would start to flow out.

Cameron says the writing doesn't have to be profound or well written— she even encourages it to be petty at times. The morning writing was a place to be heard. It was a really great way to start my day. I would often awake earlier than the kids and quietly sneak into a neighboring small guest room upstairs. I set up a desk and transformed it into my writing space.

Setting up my new space came naturally and easily. I found a desk, a swivel chair and my dad's old desk lamp in my basement. I joyfully added all sorts of personal touches: affirmations, photos, cards and notes that I had kept over the years. When we transitioned into our new home, I had diligently and thoroughly set up the kitchen and kids' bedrooms and organized the toy spaces, but I hadn't unpacked a lot of my personal belongings.

Cameron references Virginia Woolf's suggestion that every writer must have her own room, and I agree. Proudly displaying my beloved items on a cork board in my new room gave me a place to create and feel inspiration without having to leave my home. Prior to that, I had been writing in coffee shops and at the library. Now that I was creating in a space designed by me and for me, I felt a new sense of freedom and safety.

Cameron also suggests going on what she calls 'artist dates', which are intended as simple adventures to places of your choice to inspire creativity. The more obvious choices might include going to a museum or theater, but the trip could also be much simpler such as a hiking trail you have never been on or a visit to someplace new—a pet store or craft shop—that has always intrigued you. It wasn't so much about where you went, it was about opening new possibilities by going someplace new to unleash the creative spirit and be taken outside of your comfort zone.

While the kids were at school, I went on many fun trips: art galleries, farm stands, local museums, theater performances, parks and a knitting shop. These impromptu trips opened my eyes to how many creative outlets and resources were right in my own community. Occasionally, I would even take day trips into New York City and go on artist dates there. It was a fun change of pace. I now frequent all of these places on a somewhat regular basis and always look forward to expanding and discovering new spots.

The morning writing pages are recommended regardless of whether your art is painting, sculpting or music—or even if you do not engage in any of them. It turned out my art was writing. It should have been obvious, and yet, even though I had a basement full of journals, I never saw it. I was and am a writer, however I had lacked the courage and conviction to claim it.

Cameron notes that people who have difficulty spelling, or don't possess good grammar skills, think they can't be writers. Indeed, she makes the observation that many writers have poor spelling and grammar skills. I recalled essays I submitted in high school English being covered in red ink due to typos and poor grammar. As I prepared for the verbal section of the required S.A.T standardized tests, I was extremely frustrated and insecure about my abilities in this area.

If I was ever going to be serious about writing, I felt I should have college credentials to justify it. I had a doctorate degree in physical therapy. I considered going back to school for a brief moment, but I attended some writing workshops first. As it turned out, I felt incredibly intimidated being in a roomful of people trying to find their way on their creative journey—and equally intimated being around the professional writers who served as the teachers. The seed of my creativity had just been planted and had barely sprouted, and I felt I needed a fence around it to protect it, so I went back to my writing room and continued my work. The quiet was a relief, and I took refuge in the solitude. I hung photocopies of the creative affirmations and basic principles in Cameron's book on the walls. As my resistance faded away, it allowed me to hear my inner voice, and the writing started to pour out loud and clear.

As I did my writing exercises and morning pages, I would pause and stare at the words I had put up on the wall: "I am a channel for God's creativity," "Creativity is the natural order of life," "As I listen to the creator within, I am led," and "I am willing to learn to let myself create." I am so grateful to Cameron's book for giving me these affirmations and the permission to write. Several weeks later, it felt like no coincidence that I got what felt like a divine vision to write this book.

Two weeks after my vision, I was on a plane to Sedona with Ken, my sister and some friends. Although the trip had been planned a while back, the timing was perfect. I considered it an extended artist date, and it helped my vision gain momentum. Sedona's red rock vortices are thought to be swirling centers of energy that are conducive to healing, meditation and self-exploration. The term *energy vortex* was new to me, but the feeling was not. Hiking up to the breathtaking Airport Mesa, seeing the thrilling view of the blue sky and red rock all around, the peaceful but energized feeling was euphoric. It felt similar to what I had felt at the Giant's Causeway in Ireland.

Sedona's natural wonder lends itself to a vast community of energy workers, healers and psychics. Throughout the years, when I was hungry for a peek inside myself, I had had several psychic readings. Now that I felt wide-open and in the magical Southwest, it felt like the perfect time and I was eager to get a reading once again. In addition to the abundant psychic community, there are also many healing crystal shops. There were so many psychics to choose from. I tried not to overthink which one would be the right one and just picked the one at the crystal shop we were in.

I went to the back of the store, sat in the small room, and had my reading done. I still have the yellow post-it note from my reading: "100 percent on the right path, right time, right place." I smiled from ear to ear. I was so happy to have my feelings validated. I told the psychic about my vision and asked her if I would ever actually write a book. It seemed so far-fetched at the time, but to my surprise, delight and horror, she said I would, and I began to cry.

For some reason, maybe out of forgetfulness or fear, I neglected to ask her my most burning question: How long would it take? Fortunately, she had given me her email address. When I got home, I emailed her to see if she could answer my question. I was very excited when she emailed me back: "These things take time." She gave me more predictions for what she saw coming, not just as it applied to me but for all humanity as well. She said 2018 would be the year to 'clean out my closet' for the abundant new wardrobe that was coming in 2019. The closet and wardrobe were metaphors for coming face-to-face with more internal skeletons, but the rewards would be abundant expansion. Boy was she right.

Throughout the years, my childhood best friend and I have regularly seen the numeric sign 919. It most often appears on a clock, but occasionally we see it in the amount at the grocery store or on the registration sticker of a car's windshield. My friend and I used to see it when we lived in New York City together, and as we would see it on a clock and look into each other's eyes, there would be an aha moment. It felt like a message from above saying, "Stop what you are doing and realize this is all part of something so much greater." When we lived apart, we would often text each other when we noticed 919; we still do so quite regularly. The psychic's prediction of the abundant wardrobe coming in 2019 sparked a similar internal aha.

When I got back from my trip, I was on fire! I continued reading and studying *The Artist's Way* and came to a passage in the book titled 'Synchronicity', a reference to Carl Jung who defined synchronicity as meaningful coincidences. I was overjoyed that I finally had a word to describe the many fortuitous events that had transpired: the feeling that I had been energetically summoned to Hampton Bays; the cosmic treasure hunt that had led to my new therapist Lois; discovering *The Artist's Way*;

the magic of Sedona; and of course the revelation of my book vision. I know tattoos are not for everyone, and I don't feel they should be approached haphazardly, but I was so excited that I had the word *Synchronicity* tattooed on my right forearm. This decision may have seemed impulsive, but my profound feelings needed a radical expression.

Years ago, after traveling through Spain and reading *The Alchemist*, I got a tattoo of a spiral on the back of my right shoulder. I went on the trip with my now sister-in-law to celebrate having graduated from physical therapy and nursing school. I was feeling accomplished about graduating, and going to Europe for the first time was something I had always wanted to do. *The Alchemist* is a book about the realization of one's destiny, and it made me feel like I was on my way to mine. In the book, Santiago, the shepherd boy, asks how he will know if he is on the right path. He is told he will see signs along the way. I had started noticing signs myself. I was seeing spirals, and they resonated as signs telling me I was on the right path. These were signs of synchronicity before I was even aware of the term. It felt right to mark that moment of realization with a spiral tattoo then, just as a synchronicity tattoo felt like the right thing now.

As I continued writing and working on the book, I was riding high into the new year, but I was also experiencing inevitable lows. I felt fearful that I would fail and heard discouraging voices in my head. The voices said, "Who are you to write a book? Why would anyone want to read it? You aren't capable of this undertaking. What if it is terrible and you fail miserably?"

Thankfully, as I continued to write and not engage in them, the voices started to drift away. Eventually, I had been able to answer back, "Maybe I don't have a master's degree in fine arts, but who cares? I have read many books written by people who lacked an English degree, and I still enjoyed their books." I also answered back that I have a right to tell my story and do so proudly. Telling my story is not a declaration stating mine is better than anyone else's. We all have a story, and if we feel compelled to tell it through a painting, a sculpture, a song, or a book, then we should. Cameron's final rule on the list of rules of the road is "Great Creator, I will take care of the quantity, you take care of the quality." I felt like I wasn't alone. The divine inspiration that had brought the vision wanted to be made manifest. It felt bigger than just me, and that kept me going.

Another author who has guided my creative recovery is Elizabeth Gilbert. There is a quote on the cover of *The Artist's Way* from Gilbert stating, "*The Artist's Way* brings much insight, gently helping you see what is holding you back, and showing you how to move forward." I had come across Gilbert and Cameron separately, so the synchronicity of seeing these two author's names on the same cover brought a smile to my soul. Years ago, I—along with millions—were gloriously touched by Elizabeth Gilbert's best seller, *Eat Pray Love*. I even saw an audiobook recently that is a collection of personal stories by people sharing their transformative experiences after reading the book.

I had read *Eat Pray Love* while Ken and I were on vacation in the Dominican Republic. Both of us were in grad school and studying endless hours each day. We desperately wanted to take a vacation. Being in grad school, funds for a vacation were extremely limited. Somehow, we managed to pool funds and, after comparing all the travel websites, found the cheapest all-inclusive Caribbean vacation we could find. The modest resort in the Dominican Republic was just okay. It had a pool and a beach, but otherwise, it was not what I had in mind when it came to a vacation or exotic travel, so while there, I lived vicariously through Gilbert. As she traveled through Italy, India and Bali, she was on the real adventures I longed to be on. Sitting on the beach and reading about India, I declared, "One day, I will go there too."

Sure enough, a few years later, I did in fact make it to India. I was walking down a street in Bangalore and saw yet another book by Elizabeth Gilbert: *Committed: A Skeptic Makes Peace with Marriage*. I was shocked to see it! I hadn't thought of Gilbert and *Eat Pray Love* for many years, and now I was in Bangalore, India staring at another one of Gilbert's books, this one on marriage. Just recently married myself—and having overcome my own skepticism about marriage—I bought the book. Bangalore was three hours west of where I was staying in the small town of Vellore. In my rural environment, I had not been in a modern city or seen any signs of American culture in weeks. I couldn't even come close to explaining the significance of all of this to the people I was traveling with. I started to read the book on the bus as we left Bangalore.

These experiences of synchronicity with Elizabeth Gilbert were fascinating. It happened again years later in the Bridgehampton library.

I was looking for an audiobook for an upcoming trip. I saw Elizabeth Gilbert's name on a brightly colored audiobook called *Big Magic: Creative Living beyond Fear*. Our history together encouraged me to borrow it without question—even though I didn't have any plans for creative living at the time.

As I started listening to it, once again I fell in love with Gilbert's work. It felt like an old friend was telling me inspiring stories that aligned with the transformative work I had been doing. The book started with the story of an adult friend of Gilbert's who had resumed her childhood interest in ice skating and how she fell in love with it again. Gilbert made it clear that the story didn't end with her friend quitting her job and winning the Olympics, since that wasn't the point. The point was she found her passion and reconnected with it. It made me realize, creative living wasn't solely for professional painters or actors who perform Shakespeare; it was for all of us.

I had been to Sedona and had my encounter with the psychic who told me that 2018 would be the year of clearing out my closet. It was now February. My incredible husband bought me the most wonderfully romantic Valentine's Day gift ever; California Closets would come in and redesign our walk-in closet. After living in New York City for ten years, I accepted the notion of limited storage and cluttered, cramped, tiny bedroom closets. Each time we moved, we upgraded in terms of space. Our third and final apartment was a two-bedroom two-bathroom duplex! One bedroom was on the main floor for the kids, and downstairs was a big open space for Ken and me. Our new spacious apartment wasn't technically a two-bedroom place, because our room at the bottom of the stairs didn't have a door and was in the basement of the building. It also didn't have a closet, but it did have a door that went to the back of the building and led to an outside twenty-by-twenty concrete slab on which we put a hibachi and a few plants. We threw a few parties there. We were grateful for our new home with a backyard. We didn't have to leave New York, and as a bonus, my dad hung shelving in the corner nook of the downstairs space. It really felt like we were living large!

Moving to our first house in Hampton Bays, was an even greater upgrade. It was a spacious modular house, and when it was delivered from the factory, the closet space was substantial, including a walk-in closet in our master bedroom. However, the white wire shelving that came with it was very upsetting to the California Closet consultant who gasped when she walked in and said, "What a waste." When she showed me her vision of organized shelving, cubbies and specially concealed pull-out hampers, I was sold. It felt a bit extravagant and exorbitant, but the fine saleswoman justified that I would appreciate the organization and efficiency of the newly designed space multiple times a day, making it worth it. Two years later, I agree. Maybe other people would have chosen diamonds or a new car, but redesigning my closet has brought me joy and satisfaction over and over. As I dress and prepare for the day in a space that I put a lot of love, energy and money into, it makes me think back to my abundance training. It makes me feel really good.

Although I felt the purchase was justified, I figured it made sense to shave a few dollars off the price and decided to empty, spackle and paint the closet myself in preparation for the installation. I recruited my parents to assist me. My dad removed the white wire shelving and spackled the holes, then he left, and my mom and I began painting. As we peacefully rolled the white paint on the walls of my emptied-out closet, transforming the space, my mom and I had a heart-to-heart conversation that I will remember for the rest of my life.

For years, my mom had spared me the pain of her initial undiagnosed battle with postpartum depression. I was my mom's first pregnancy. She went into labor, but then she had a cesarean section. After the birth, although she felt the joy of having a new baby, she also felt incredible depression in a time that postpartum depression was less understood and acknowledged than it is now.

It took a year and a half before she found a doctor who identified what she was going through. He was able to prescribe medication for her which brought huge relief. I will spare the rest of the details for the sake of her privacy, but the clarity and connectedness of the conversation I had with my mother that day as we painted the closet was groundbreaking. To some degree, I had always known some of this information, but the lighthearted front my mom puts up most of the time never allowed me to question her about her struggles. In spite of what she was going through, she did the best she could to keep it together: going to work, keeping a tidy home, making sure we had new clothes for school and filled stockings at Christmas.

Time and time again, it never ceases to amaze me what other people are carrying around inside themselves. Having sensed my mom's struggle, I had always longed to question her about it further, but had refrained because I had not wanted to inflict any unnecessary pain on her. Now that I had experienced birth and the stress of having a new baby, I was able to relate to my mom's experience in a way I hadn't before. As we talked, she got emotional. My mom stated that after giving birth to both my sister and I via cesarean sections, each time the post-surgical aftermath had led to nursing difficulties. She then shared how, after seeing me nurse Eliza for the first time, she experienced the physical feelings of a nursing letdown response in her own breasts. Seeing her daughter and granddaughter connect was a breakthrough moment. She was finally able to feel something that had eluded her before. The connection between the mind and body goes so deep, and this was certainly an example. Awakening was occurring, and it wasn't even spring yet.

As the psychic had suggested, my closet was literally and figuratively being cleared out. The awakening I was experiencing was thrilling and empowering. After years of transformational work and therapy, I was finally figuring things out. I felt like a surfer, cool and calm on my board, in the tranquil ocean of my life. But just as I reached some stability, a new destabilizing wave came.

As all of this was taking place, Ken saw his nephrologist for a routine visit. During this visit, the doctor advised resuming the transplant evaluation process we had put on pause seven years ago. It took a while for the news to sink in; the transplant could no longer wait! And just like that, the calm waters turned turbulent. One after another, a series of new waves began to materialize. The highs and lows were intense. There were extreme shifts affecting my mood and energy. One day, I would be in bed due to the fatigue and feelings of depression, and the next day, I felt euphoric. This came as a surprise, sort of, until I began to realize these waves were keeping me flexible and alert. Ultimately, what was being set in motion—what I sensed was about to happen—was an essential part of the journey of growth and expansion I had signed up for.

If I wanted to avoid the oncoming waves, I should get out of the ocean. My response to that was, hell no! I'd rather keep falling off and getting back on than get out. Yes, I would often cling to the concept of calm waters, but on some level, I must admit I came to appreciate the thrill of the journey I was on. I was on the transformational superhighway, and breakdowns and breakthroughs were coming in fast. One day I would break down and think I was going crazy, then the next day a breakthrough would come. This process continued throughout the year, and it all felt significant.

To complicate things further, and perhaps as an unconscious means of distraction, I was also spending a lot of time researching the possibility of homeschooling my children. As much as I liked their new school, I was still in withdrawal and dearly missing Waldorf education. My obvious passion for Waldorf and the hours I spent studying it, made me think I could take matters into my own hands. I worked diligently, meeting with homeschooling parents and researching homeschool curriculums and laws.

I tried to keep it all in perspective. The decision of whether or not to homeschool was gnawing at me. It felt like an unconventional thing to do. I felt a pit in my stomach, but something inside of me said just keep going with it and see how it plays out. I worried about how the kids would adjust. I also wondered if I could actually pull off being both their parent and their teacher. Also, how would the upcoming transplant fit into all of this?

By June, the process resolved on its own, and I couldn't be happier with how it all turned out. I had looked into forming homeschooling co-ops, working with other parents, doing it all on my own, and even starting a first grade at our former school. I came across a lot of homeschooling resources right in our own community, and in the end, I gained a lot of clarity. I surrendered and reenrolled them in their current school. Having gone through the process, and knowing I had left no stone unturned put my mind at ease. As it turned out, I wouldn't have had it any other way. Looking back, I have no regrets. In the process, I had gained great respect for homeschooling and the dedicated parents who make it work. I had even reconnected with a friend from childhood I had lost touch with over the years. I reached out to her because I had heard she was homeschooling her family. Six months later, when the following September came—a month after the all-consuming transplant—I was relieved I hadn't started in on a new venture like that.

Deciding whether to homeschool or not had been another opportunity to confront an old pattern—the pattern of perfectionism. Growing up, my mom kept our home in perfect order. We still laugh about the pink-handled brush she kept discreetly hidden next to the rug in our dining room, which she used to brush the tassels into perfect order. My dad, for his part, was a skilled builder and relied on his high standards of perfection to ensure his customers got a product that was solid and lasting. I, on the other hand, wasn't as concerned if the sheets in my linen closet weren't neatly folded or my kids' clothes weren't perfectly clean. I didn't feel that same need for perfection my parents felt. Or did I? It started to occur to me that I actually was a perfectionist, who, at the same time, was always trying to resist the torture of maintaining a perfect image of myself.

A while back, I had a craniosacral therapy session. The practitioner clears away and releases tension deep in the body to improve health and function. This particular practitioner also combines her intuitive abilities and connections with spirit to bring deeper healing. While she was working on me, she shared a message she received from her spirit guides about me needing to release perfection. Initially, the message had come as a surprise to me. I didn't have a type A personality, nor did I think I came off as a perfectionist. As I continued to contemplate and look deeper, I realized my perfection came in a more subtle form. It was a deeper need to do the right thing, act the right way, learn a new skill effortlessly, be very efficient with my time, and live with perfect equanimity of emotion.

I can recall wanting to be recognized as a well-behaved child by holding in any darkness or dysfunction. This trend continued throughout the years. These tendencies were vividly on display when I became a mother: trying to maintain my patience, having my children avoid screens, trying to filter the adult world from them, trying to maintain a perfect sense of rhythm to our days, and more. I maintain my belief in these concepts because I deeply believe in their value. However, the perfect execution of it all—while also trying to be a good person, which I defined as not letting anyone down—was hard to live up to. The pressure of my perfect expectations of myself had nothing to do with anyone else. It never had anything to do with comparisons—most of the time. I wasn't trying to be the perfect mom or person. I was simply afraid of falling short of my own self-imposed beliefs and standards.

This was evident in the educational journey I was on. I clearly loved Waldorf education for the value it brought to my children and myself, and

I will always advocate on behalf of it. However, it wasn't available to me anymore, and it was hard letting go; at times, it still is. A conscious parent's wish for an outside-the-box approach seemed to be a progression to a desire for perfection. The refusal to let go, clinging to an idea of perfection, these were hallmarks of my need to meet unreachably high standards. Eventually, I broke through and overcame these tendencies, but this need for perfection is a continual challenge that requires ongoing vigilance.

The issue of how best to school my children resolved itself, when, a few days later, I got an email from the school informing the parents who the teachers would be for the next school year. I was amazed to see that my daughters would both be having their same teachers we had loved from last year. I am glad that instead of forcing myself to stop the process, it lost momentum on its own. Like pushing a heavy boulder uphill, I felt the universe clearly telling me to stop pushing. I just stepped aside and allowed the surrender. This brought about a sense of freedom.

When this season of change began, little did I know what all of this clearing of closets and confronting my need to be perfect (while not looking perfect) was preparing me for. There had been many breakthroughs this year. It had started in February and continued all spring and into the summer. I had cleared out my closet and started preparing for one of the biggest events we would ever have to go through. The unknowns we would be facing as we approached the coming transplant before us were scary. However, the previous years of studying my favorite authors' works, as well as breakthrough trainings, trips abroad, and my creative recovery all felt like they were occurring in perfect order, preparing me with a strong foundation and sense of self that would serve me well—no matter what life would bring.

I've heard it said, "If the roots are strong, the tree needn't worry about the wind." I had already felt strong, but now I was doing the necessary inner work that would deepen those roots and clear away the emotional distractions, obstacles and habits in order to help guide me through this next phase—and beyond.

# CHAPTER 5

# A Different Kind of Hamptons Summer

I always find it amazing how tears come with sadness, happiness, laughter, and a myriad of other emotions. My tears often materialize without warning at moments I don't expect: parent-teacher conferences, graduations (even if I don't know anyone who is graduating), weddings and other deeply significant moments. I guess that is in part due to my empathic nature. An empath is someone who is highly sensitive to what others around them are feeling.

I can often feel the emotions of others and as a result feel deep and profound emotions myself. I notice how uncomfortable it can make the person staring at my tears feel, and I often conceal them for the sake of that person's discomfort. On an old *Seinfeld* episode, George Costanza said "As she started crying, she was like a fire—and all I wanted to do was put her out."

I wish the person on the other side would put their arm around me and tell me to let it out, or just silently slip away with a smile and let my tears burn like the kind of therapeutic forest fires that park rangers allow. Tears are emotions that are being cleansed out of the body and people should stand up and cheer when someone is crying. I like to think it is celebratory to let your tears out versus repressing the feelings inside your soul. Crying allows a release or letting go of the emotions versus repressing them and storing them.

I think we should also encourage the crying person's vulnerability and openness. I get so disturbed by how we hide our feelings and then switch to conversations about the weather or the news. I would always rather discuss the deeper underlying concerns rather than superficial attempts at meaningless conversation. However, the discussion of feelings comes with the stipulation that both parties show some sort of willingness to address the situation, which is why avoidance is so common.

In my younger days, I would sit at the other end of a phone conversation, listening and feeling the pain and complaints from a person who had no intention of taking responsibility, or of looking at themselves and honestly addressing the situation at hand. My empathic skin has toughened through lots of work and tools. I do not take on people's pain to the degree I used to.

*The Empath's Survival Guide* by Judith Orloff and *The Highly Sensitive Person* by Elaine Aron have helped me diagnose and treat myself. I've learned to set boundaries and remove myself from painful conversations—except if it comes with some version of acknowledgment.

The ideal language would be, 'I am suffering, and once I let it out, I am willing to take action, go within and find the deeper meaning to all of this.' Of course, it rarely sounds like that. However, I can usually hear and feel a person's willingness, which is where the gold of transformation lies. At the end of the day, a good cry feels like a shower for my inner self. Afterward, I come out feeling refreshed and liberated—along with a headache as a reminder of the passage of the cleansed emotion.

Memorial Day weekend of 2018 brought a mixture of emotions that resulted in a lot of tears. The end of May in Hampton Bays is often cooler than inland New York City. The ocean hasn't warmed up yet from the spring, but this does not stop the beachgoers from New York City, New Jersey, and elsewhere from flooding in after waiting all year to return to their beloved memories of summertime bliss and a beach-or-bust mentality.

Luckily, this year, Friday brought a lovely seventy-degree day. Saturday too was a day to remember down by the bay. A minimal breeze made it tolerable to take a refreshing plunge into the mid-sixties Peconic Bay. The kids played in the stream at one of our local bay beaches, and the euphoria in the air gave way to a beautiful afternoon backyard party at our house.

Our family and a few close friends gathered to celebrate my older daughter Eliza's seventh birthday. Eliza had requested an origami-themed party, so I spent the earlier part of the week constructing decorative garland from origami animals that both my daughters had made. I often find handwork, and this kind of party preparation, therapeutic. I love looking at the delicate beauty of the paper figures and the zen-like process of watching my children make them.

On Saturday, I was blissfully preparing by cleaning up the yard. It felt like absolute synchronicity to open the mailbox and find a huge book called *A Course in Miracles.* I lifted the heavy blue textbook and embraced it. A dear friend knew this book had entered my consciousness and sent it to me as a gift.

A few weeks prior, the 2018 Hay House Summit had come around again as it does every May. By signing up with your email, you gain access to hundreds of free talks and lessons from Hay House authors on self-help, health and wellness, angels, psychic abilities, Feng Shui, essential oils, and more—in addition to the good old ones from Louise Hay, Esther Hicks, and Wayne Dyer. I listened to a talk on miracles by Gabrielle Bernstein. The talk focused on inviting miracles into your life, and in a short meditation/visualization, you ask for a miracle in an area in your life that is a problem on a big or small level. I asked for a miracle around finding a new home for my chickens.

My girls had come to love our chickens and picked them up and often played with them during outside time in our backyard. In a recent visit with Ken's nephrologist, he gave us some information about what to expect from the transplant and the postsurgical regimen of immunosuppressive medication to help ensure my donated kidney was not rejected by his body. Initially, the immunosuppression would be high, in turn making the infection risk high. This medication regimen came with the prohibition of being in crowded public spaces, eating raw foods like sushi (and the clams we loved to catch), runny yolk eggs (which Ken loved), caution with eating raw vegetables—making sure they are thoroughly washed, and avoiding salad bars and food where freshness is in question. One of the medications in the regimen also makes you photosensitive so he advised limited sun exposure. As I was contemplating all of the lifestyle changes that would have to be made, I asked about our chickens. The doctor advised getting rid of them due to the risk of infection they would bring. We were willing to comply for the sake of Ken's health, but as a parent I dreaded upsetting and disappointing my children. There were also the logistics of getting rid of five chickens.

Since it was only the end of May, I figured we could enjoy them for the rest of the summer and break the news a few weeks prior to the transplant. However, this weighed on me heavily. I used visualization to envision a miracle for my chicken dilemma. Coincidently, the next day, I went to a plant sale at the farm where I had gotten the chickens. I shared my dilemma with the farm owner, and she said her farm was more than filled, but she was in the process of trying to start a new farm across town. If it worked out, she would happily take them there. I was overjoyed! I hadn't even planned on going to the plant sale. I heard about it at the last minute. It was a miracle. A new home for our chickens, right here in our town, with a woman who raises and sells chickens for a living. This miracle of the chicken relocation, showed me that miracles were possible. Even though it wasn't a firm agreement, and might fall through later, it felt like the universe had heard me. That comforted me and soothed a very deep fear I had been harboring: the outcome of the transplant.

This situation made me want to learn more about *A Course in Miracles*. I looked it up online, discovered an app, and downloaded it. From listening to various talks throughout the years, I had heard the giant book referenced and even seen it on a friend's bookshelf and in the library. Due to its overwhelming size, I didn't feel I was ready to undertake it. With the app, I started reading the introduction: "This is a course in miracles. It is a required course. Only the time you take it is voluntary." Right away, I got chills. This was indeed my time. The book goes on to say, "Nothing real can be threatened. Nothing unreal exists. Herein lies the peace of God." The nothing real and unreal part resonated deeply, but the mention of God made me uncomfortable.

As a kid, I had gone to a Lutheran church with my mom from time to time, received my First Communion and was even confirmed at a Presbyterian church. That was the extent of my relationship with a church and unfortunately, with God. Later on, after doing yoga for many years and taking yoga teacher training, I called yoga my religion due to the spiritual nature of this practice to which I had become very dedicated. Years later, I started following Louise Hay and Esther Hicks. They both made references to the terms *universe* and *source energy*. Those terms resonated with me. I believed in a higher power, but the term *God* came with religious dogma I had learned about in Sunday school, which never quite suited my beliefs. *Universe* and *source energy* were pleasant terms that felt less threatening and eased my resistance so I could continue with my work and not have to tackle my issues with the term *God*. I was ready to plunge into *A Course in Miracles,* but I had to get past the word *God*. I decided to temporarily make peace with the word, study the course, and see where it got me.

My daughter's party was wonderful. It was an all-American post-beach barbecue, Hamptons style, with rosé, quinoa, and Pellegrino. We served clams we had harvested from the bay the previous day. We had a treasure hunt, played our favorite backyard game, Can Jam, and ate ice cream cake. I loved watching the children run around with our chickens. I'll never forget seeing my four-year-old, dressed in a beautiful navy blue halter dress with a brown belt that my sister had gotten for her, running around with our brown Araucana chicken, Cheeper Jumper, under her arm. I was filled with joy.

Yet the joy gave way to sorrow. Although the rest of the weekend was also filled with fun times, fishing, beach volleyball, and delicious dinners at our favorite restaurants overlooking the water, I spent Monday and most of Tuesday crying. It would be a very different kind of summer, and that perfect BBQ scene would probably be the one and only of the season. At the next party, our beloved chickens would be absent. The summer of 2018 was not going to be our typical Hamptons summer filled with visits from New York City friends, sunsets, bike rides, and sunburns. This summer was filled with preparation plans for the upcoming transplant.

I should go back. Ken was born with a rare genetic kidney disorder called Dent's disease. This disorder was apparent by evidence of protein in his urine, and he had been under the care of a nephrologist since he was a child. Initially, they did not know the cause of his kidney dysfunction, but they knew at some point his kidneys would fail and require transplantation. At age six, he had his first kidney biopsy. At age fourteen, he had an unrelated episode of pericarditis (inflammation of tissue surrounding the heart). The cause of this was unknown and possibly viral in nature. He was experiencing shortness of breath and chest pain after a freshman football game and was subsequently hospitalized. He required a surgical pericardial window and chest tube placement to remove excess fluid around the heart and lungs. Afterward he was treated with nonsteroidal anti-inflammatory drugs (NSAIDs) and antibiotics, which further damaged his kidneys.

Since his kidneys were unable to tolerate the NSAIDs, he required episodes of prednisone/steroid therapy to keep the inflammation of the pericardium down. He had to manage all the associated side effects that come with steroids. At age nineteen, after multiple unsuccessful attempts to lower the steroids, he required another surgical procedure called pericardial stripping. Thankfully, this procedure was successful. A few years later, he was able to go off all the steroids completely. His cardiac function was normal and he didn't require any further cardiac care. His kidneys continued to fail and were monitored by his highly respected pediatric nephrologist from then on. As serious as it was, Ken was otherwise healthy. It's worth noting that those episodes were unable to penetrate his humorous and lighthearted nature. He spent his twenties and most of his thirties living a relatively normal life: graduating from college and medical school, completing his residency, traveling, playing sports, and spending fun times with his loved ones.

When Ken's pediatric nephrologist, who practiced at Columbia Presbyterian Hospital in New York City, retired, he referred him to a new nephrologist. Ken started seeing Dr. J when I was pregnant with Eliza. Ken's new highly respected nephrologist, who was also at Columbia, planted the seed that the transplant was coming, but we did not know when. More than seven years had passed, and after careful consideration and much collaboration with the wonderful team of health care professionals, we decided to go forward with the procedure. As fate would have it, our blood types matched. I would be the donor.

In addition to going to the beach and taking the kids to swim lessons, there were also many trips to New York City to see social workers, surgeons, nephrologists, psychologists, transplant coordinators, financial coordinators and nutritionists. Ken and I both also required a thorough battery of diagnostic tests, EKGs, CT scans and blood draws. It was all consuming, but we were fortunate enough to have the help and the support we needed to fit it all into our lives without too much drama.

We celebrated July 4, 2018 with fireworks on the beach. Five days later, my youngest daughter, Maddy turned five. She and Eliza kept us busy and distracted, so life felt relatively normal. We spent most of our time with the girls and asked our family and friends not to discuss the coming surgeries around them. We felt this was best for Eliza and Maddy, but it was also helpful for Ken and I. We were facing the music, and coping, but didn't want to wallow in it excessively.

When the children were not around, there were some emotional conversations with friends and family members, and the reality would resurface. The support was great, but I wanted to avoid the shocked faces and conversations. I started to retreat and turn inward. Life was so busy, but when there was downtime and the kids were at their grandparents' house, or I could find a moment, I would try to quiet down and tune out the external world. I would tune in to myself and try to stay strong and connected by going for walks on the beach, meditating and writing. Writing was especially helpful. I was so grateful I had this creative outlet to help me cope with all the thoughts and feelings inside my head and my body.

During this time, energy clearing work was also an extremely helpful coping tool. My cousin would conduct distant energy clearing/healing sessions over the phone. She would use a combination of energy therapies, including Tong Ren. Integrating elements of Traditional Chinese Medicine, the Tong Ren practitioner directs chi (energy) to blockage points by tapping a lightweight magnetic hammer on a small anatomical model of the human body, which serves as a representation of the patient.

Another therapy used during the distant healing sessions was spiritual response therapy (SRT). SRT works on a spiritual level to help eliminate spiritual, mental, emotional and physical challenges with the use of a pendulum and special charts. SRT works with your "higher self" by searching the subconscious mind and soul records to find discordant, limiting ideas and replacing them with loving, supportive ideas and beliefs.

Reiki was another form of energy healing I found helpful. Reiki transfers "universal energy" from the practitioner to the patient. With guidance and training, I was even able to practice Reiki on myself. Working with my cousin on this energy clearing work helped me release any negative emotions I was holding onto in association with the upcoming transplant. Lying in my bed during our phone sessions, I would go within myself and feel deeply connected to my higher guidance system.

Another healer, Tracey, did distant craniosacral and medium healing work over the phone. I had worked with Tracey a while back and had a breakthrough session on releasing perfection. This time, Tracey tapped into a message from my grandfather on my dad's side who died when I was five. The message was to "believe in my bones". The message had come through her, and it was up to me to uncover the meaning. I began to feel a new ease in my bones—maybe for the first time in my life—and a belief that everything would be okay. I felt really empowered. I was going deep within myself and beyond. The higher realms were guiding me. This wasn't a dysfunctional situation; it was all part of a bigger cosmic plan.

I was gaining a stronger connection to a higher power and I was getting a little more comfortable reading *A Course in Miracles*. The course helped deepen my faith. Maybe all of this sounded far-fetched, but it felt like the absolute truth, which I was realizing was all that mattered. My old limiting beliefs were having less power over me and I felt I was strengthening the muscles of my inner self.

My cousin recommended yet another energy worker, and I was receptive. Julie did intuitive readings over the phone. I went to a beach not far from my house so my kids wouldn't distract me and called Julie. I gave her very little personal information, but I told her about the upcoming transplant. She read me like a book—even though we had never met. Julie said she saw water. I told her that I lived in Hampton Bays and was sitting on a beach staring at the bay. She said how good water was for me and how it grounded me. I laughed and told her I swim almost every day in the summer and that I meditate by the water to ground myself and create a peaceful calm feeling.

Julie confirmed that where I was living was perfect for me, which didn't surprise me. I had felt energetically summoned to live in Hampton Bays. She said that my spirit guides were deep within me and literally wrapped around my organs. They were guiding and protecting me. I burst into tears and told her I was scared of what was coming. Still, even so, deep down, I had never felt stronger, safer or more secure. I felt like I had energetic allies. This experience combined with all the other work I was doing was really setting the stage I was about to walk onto. My psychic closet felt all cleared out, and every shelf and hidden space had been dusted and thoroughly cleaned.

Through the Advanced Training Workshop, the Abundance Workshop, the Hay House authors' talks and my travels, I was further discovering who I was. I started to realize how much I relied on my own self for strength to get through challenging times. Going back to my perfectionist nature, I would get frustrated if I had a bad day or if I succumbed to difficult situations. I was taking the next step of connecting to a higher power and surrendering to it when I felt challenged. I was reaching out and asking for help. My session with Julie was so helpful. I realized I didn't have to do it all alone. Supernatural forces were assisting and guiding me at all times. All I had to do was shed my resistance and tap into it. It was such a relief and was very reassuring to have this nonphysical support guiding me.

As I was going deeper within, my intuition was getting stronger and clearer. My inner voice is highly intuitive, but in the past, it was hard to hear and feel. The mind chatter that my ego was always playing was like a loud broken record. Deep down, I always felt I was intuitive. This ability to connect ran deep in our family lineage, but I never really declared it at the risk of sounding pompous or crazy.

It was definitely more apparent after the passing of my Aunt Madeleine. As tragic as her passing was, I remember looking at the sun and feeling her smile at me and feeling a deep sense of peace. One day shortly after her passing, with tears in my eyes, I shared a vision with my mom. I told her I had seen my aunt in the bathroom where she had been violently murdered. Her head was resting on an archangel's lap. The archangel was gently stroking her hair and saying, "Don't worry. It will be over soon, and you will then be one with pure positive energy." This made me feel, with absolute certainty, that there had been a peaceful passing, despite the evidence the authorities shared with us. My aunt's passing brought more visions and also the sightings of owls. Incredibly, others who knew my aunt were also seeing owls. A friend of my aunt saw an owl when she visited my aunt's house after the incident. My sister and I have always shared the intuitive owl as our spirit animal. After my aunt's passing, all the associated synchronicity led us to get matching owl tattoos, mine on my forearm and my sisters on the top of her foot.

After my uncle died, I also had visitation dreams from him. In many of those dreams we were at family gatherings in his house. In the way a medium channels energy through a conduit, I also felt him talking to me as we traveled through the African savanna. It didn't surprise me that he was there and everywhere else watching over our family. These intuitive connections were especially strong when I was in powerful natural surroundings, such as the inlet in Hampton Bays, the Giant's Causeway, and the African savanna. All of these intuitive experiences were helpful to me as I began to face Ken's surgery and my part in it.

On our many visits to the hospital, we asked the transplant team if it would be possible to have the surgery in early August. The kids would be out of school, and our summer schedule was relatively freer. The transplant coordinator shuffled through our thick files and thought it would probably work, but couldn't guarantee it. Scheduling a kidney transplant isn't like scheduling a dental cleaning. Scheduling and completing the screening visits would take time. Once the long list of visits and tests was completed, the case would be presented to a selection committee. They would decide if Ken would get his surgery. We felt our case would likely be selected since we met the basic criteria: Ken was healthy enough to undergo the surgery, he was compliant with the medication regimen, we had strong social support and we were financially stable. So, even though our case would most likely get selected, the question of *when* remained.

On a hot July morning, the girls and I were painting at our backyard picnic table when I finally got the phone call I was waiting for. The transplant coordinator said, "Good news—your surgery is scheduled for August 1". It took me a moment to catch my breath. I had been waiting for so long to get a date. We knew it was coming, but without a date being set, it didn't feel real. Now in this moment, it couldn't have felt more real. In two and a half weeks, the event that had been in the back of our minds for more than seven years would finally occur.

I hung up the phone and called Ken. He had been busy at work all summer. He was working extra to make up for the New York City evaluation visits. Even as he was tending to his own medical needs, he was giving clinical care to patients. I told him the transplant was scheduled, and after a long pause, he said, "Shit, I guess I better tell my boss."

And so, just like that, the scramble began. There was a lot of planning that had not been done yet because we hadn't known for sure when and if the transplant was really going to happen. There were practical matters to be dealt with. During the day, I was visiting, calling and emailing farms to relocate our chickens. The other arrangement had fallen through. At night, I looked for apartments on Craigslist and Airbnb that were within walking distance of the hospital. There would be many postoperative follow up visits, and we would need to be close by.

It was a crazy time. I was frantic but calm and filled with equal amounts of fear and hope. My energy work and higher power connections kept me grounded and strong. However, it was an ongoing process. The day-to-day details of life and caring for the kids drained me. My head filled with new fears. I meditated to help organize my thoughts and keep my head clear.

Since he would be out of work for two months, Ken was working late and trying to tie up loose ends. The inevitable date of August 1 was coming fast. For other people, life went on with summertime happy hours and oysters. For Ken and me, this time of year that had always felt so fun, light and familiar now felt uncharacteristically foreign.

It was hard to break the news about the surgeries to my five and seven-year-olds. I told them their dad needed a new kidney, and I was going to give him mine. Not having any insight or experience to what this entailed, they didn't really respond much. I gave them a very simple explanation, but since it didn't affect their present moment, they quickly moved back to whatever they were playing with.

Thankfully, as hard as it all was, the main course of pain came with a heaping side order of ease. I found another home for our chickens across the street from where our daughters attended school. I could console their crying with the comfort that we could visit our beloved feathery family members whenever we wanted to.

Having found a new home for the chickens, I waited a few more days to break the news to the girls, and it definitely elicited a big response. They both cried a lot. It was really hard seeing my children so sad. However, I told myself to breathe and let them get it all out. I held them and said, "I know it is sad. We will miss them." I allowed their tears to flow. My maternal instincts kicked in. I wanted to fix the situation and stop the tears by any means necessary—yelling or bribing them with ice cream or toys—but I was steadfast.

After twenty minutes or so, I said, "Dad's health is more important". I started to tear up and said, "I am doing everything I can". They stopped crying. I often held back my tears in front of my children to avoid burdening them with my sorrows, but in that moment I let them see me cry. They seemed very surprised. Afterward, we all hugged—and, miraculously, that was the end of it.

I told the girls we had one more week to enjoy the chickens before they moved to their new home. I was amazed how calm they became. We discussed the relocation process as a family. We allowed them to weigh in on the day, Saturday or Sunday, and on which cage or container we would use to transport them. Being included seemed to put them at ease.

On Saturday morning, Ken and I asked the girls if they wanted to come to the farm to drop them off or would they prefer to go to Grandma's house. Surprisingly, they wanted to go to Grandma's house. We put the chickens in the back of the pickup truck, and before we dropped the kids off, they said their goodbyes. Afterward, we dropped the chickens at their new home on the farm, and that was the end of it. We had put the old roughed-up chicken coop in the front yard of our house for someone to take, and when we got home it was gone—solving the last hassle of how to break down and get rid of the coop. Even though it was not exactly how I originally planned it, the miracle I had envisioned did in fact manifest.

Finding a place to stay in New York eventually worked out as well, even though it was definitely a struggle. I was constantly checking my email to see if any responses to my inquiries had come. I finally found a furnished sublet in Washington Heights. It was close to the hospital, was big enough to fit all four of us, was available during the dates we needed, and was in our price range. It is always hard to tell with online pictures, but it seemed to be a fit. It unsettled me to think about living in someone else's space—but I booked it.

As good fortune would have it, we were compatible with the Airbnb host whose apartment we would be renting. Getting to know her was reassuring. While we were staying at her place, she would be staying in Sag Harbor for the month of August. She was coming out to the Hamptons the week before the booking, giving us the opportunity to meet in person. We met at the Southampton Jitney stop. The Jitney is a bus line that transports people back-and-forth between New York City and the Hamptons. After our meeting, so many of my fears were resolved. She was going to be working as an art teacher at a summer program I was familiar with, and we even had a mutual friend who worked there. As if all this wasn't amazing enough, she told me her father had been a nephrologist before he passed, and she was very familiar with the nephrology department at Columbia-Presbyterian.

At that moment, I felt in alignment with the universe. Everything was falling into place.

What had felt like an unbroken trail through the raw and savage woods, now felt like a freshly paved road that was ready for travel to places unknown. It was scary, but the ride was starting to feel surprisingly smooth. We spent our final days packing and preparing for the month we would be away from home.

Two days before the transplant, on a sunny Saturday morning, we did what amounted to a reverse commute to New York City. As we drove west on the Long Island Expressway toward the city, we saw congestion going the other way. The weekenders were headed east to the Hamptons for their beach getaways. We were listening to the audiobook *The Little House on the Prairie.* Pa, Ma, Mary, Laura and baby Carrie were traveling to the undiscovered land out West in a covered wagon, while our family of four ventured to the city in our white Toyota Highlander. We were ready to face the transplant.

Me, 5 years old, with my parents.

My younger sister, Allison, and me, outside our house in Paramus, New Jersey. We had just moved in. I was 9. My sister was 5.

Here I am on the side of the road while my best friend and I were driving out west in my fully packed Toyota Corolla. I was fascinated by the wide-open spaces.

Life of a mother with two young children, chaotic but deeply gratifying.

The note the psychic wrote during our session in Sedona shortly after I got the premonition to write this book. Seeing her write these words was so reassuring.

Ken and me the evening before the kidney transplant. We walked over 100 blocks along the Hudson River path down the West Side of Manhattan. It was scary facing the unknown, but together we knew we could get through anything life threw our way.

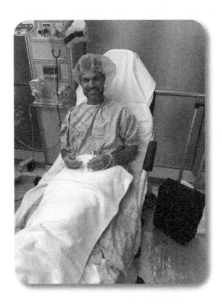

Ken, the morning of the surgery, all prepped and ready to go—always with a smile, and strong in trying times.

Ken, myself and our daughters Labor Day weekend, a little over a month after the surgery. It was triumphant. We had made it through the summer in NYC and were back home on the beach.

Ken and me at the hospital gala nine months after the transplant, feeling transformed and fabulous.

The Forest Monastery in Sri Lanka.

# CHAPTER 6

# Labor Day

August 1, 2018, the day of the surgery, was a Wednesday, and on Friday, a little more than forty-eight hours after the transplant, I was discharged from the hospital. Ken was in rough, but stable, condition and would be discharged on Saturday. Initially, when I was booking and paying for the Airbnb apartment, it had felt like a luxury. As I was being wheeled to the hospital's grand exit in a wheelchair and slowly walked the four blocks (with a friend escorting me) to our temporary home, there was no question in my mind that the choice to live within walking distance of the hospital was a medical necessity. Since Ken couldn't yet handle ambulating those four blocks, he would have to be driven. It didn't seem possible that the day before the surgery, Ken and I had enjoyed a beautiful evening excursion. We walked more than one hundred blocks down along the Hudson River, finally stopping for a relaxed supper at Ellington in the Park on 105th Street.

The thought of sitting in a car for more than two hours (without traffic) to go to the Hamptons, only to come back a few days later for the first follow up visit, would have been impossible. Ken was barely able to tolerate the car seat belt against his painful incision. This again reiterated how grateful I was that I had booked an apartment near the hospital. And though the streets of Washington Heights were tough, they had little effect on the healing oasis we had found in our sublet on the sixth floor of our prewar elevator building.

Despite the superior care at the hospital, being in our new temporary home was truly 'what the doctor ordered'. Because we were discharged at different times, and because we both required postoperative care, the social workers prohibited us from being designated caregivers for each other. We were each required to have our own caregiver while we were recuperating, which we did. Even so, with New York City delivery services and the convenience of everything being so close, we were able to manage mostly on our own. We were thankful to be getting by and declined most of the generous help that was offered—the one exception being the jugs of drinking water that were too heavy to carry. Our amazing friends and family handled those immediately by bringing and even shipping them to us.

I felt like Ken and I were getting a preview of our retirement years. During this period of recuperation and healing, we did not have the strength or stamina we were used to, but—together and very slowly—we were getting by. We would toss and turn at night and sleep during the day. We watched endless hours of movies. We were careful not to laugh too hard, since it would hurt our incisions. I won't even talk about sneezing!

As a PT, I insisted on following a walking program, and Ken eagerly complied. In the mornings, we took short walks around the neighborhood before the humidity took over the city. Later in the day, when the heat broke, we would enjoy the returning breezes on a second walk. We had follow-up visits with our doctors, and Ken was given a calendar to keep track of his numerous appointments. We would walk from our apartment to New York Presbyterian. It felt like returning to the scene of the crime.

There were biweekly appointments for Ken to get blood work to monitor his immunosuppressive medication levels, visits with his transplant nephrologist, and follow-up visits with his surgeon. I was progressing well and had only two follow-up visits with my wonderful surgeon, who then discharged me. Ken was still experiencing a lot of pain, and his functional status was quite limited. Despite the slow pace, we were encouraged by the visits. The doctors said we were both recovering well, and although we were limited, our spirits and hopes were high.

By the end of the first week, the pain was alleviating and our function was improving. Sharing organs and healing together, we never felt closer. I felt like we could get through anything. As it had been in the past, our partnership was tested with the arrival of our children.

Our daughters had stayed with Ken's parents in New Jersey until a week after the surgery. We saw them once during this time. They came to the hospital the day after the surgery to visit us and then went back to New Jersey. Although my in-laws had offered to watch them longer, speaking to the kids on the phone almost daily, I could hear they were itching to come stay with us in New York. Ken and I missed them terribly, but we were weak and barely up to the task of caring for them. I also worried if seeing us in the condition we were in would upset them.

When they finally arrived, the girls were so excited to be living in New York City. They loved experiencing the neighborhood with its numerous delis and playgrounds within walking distance. They enjoyed going out and returning home via an elevator, which was a new experience for them. They hardly noticed the Steri-Strips on our incisions or the amount of time we spent in bed and on the couch. We started out taking it slow, which was the only way to survive. We played board games on the couch, played with toys we had brought from home and with presents we had received from visiting family and friends. We enjoyed reading and knitting, but eventually it was time to get out. We started with a short trip to the playground. It was half a block away on Riverside Drive. It wasn't fancy, but it had shade from the trees and a small sprinkler that gave relief to the ninety-degree days. It was close to home if someone needed to get back. It also had frequent visits from a pushcart ice cream man who would announce his arrival with an old school rubber bike horn.

I was grateful the girls enjoyed these simple pleasures because it was all we were able to provide at the time. At five and seven, it was blissful for them. They were able to ride their scooters on paved sidewalks, which we did not have in our neighborhood in Hampton Bays. A few days later, we went to a children's museum on St. Nicholas Avenue and 155th Street. I was not ready to walk the twelve blocks to the museum, so we took an Uber. Ken could not go due to the infection risk of public places. For the girls and I, it was very empowering to go beyond the two-block radius of the last few days. In no time, we worked our way up to taking subway rides to other parts of the West Side of Manhattan. Since he was prohibited from taking public transportation, Ken would stay back. Being the trouper he was, in the mornings he would take the girls to the corner playground and to breakfast at the diner, two blocks away, so I could sleep in and rest up for our afternoon subway journeys.

By the next week, Ken was able to walk to his twice-weekly appointments four blocks away at Columbia, and to take the girls to the other playgrounds a little further away. If we had been home in Hampton Bays, he would have been unable to drive or do yard work or enjoy any of his usual leisure activities such as water sports, fishing and golf. By contrast, in the city he was able to be independent, able to get to his appointments, and could get himself a sandwich at the bodega, which was liberating. Years ago, when we were living in Manhattan, we had dreaded being in the hot city in the summer and longed for beach days out on the island, but now, recovering from our surgeries, being in the city was perfect.

We continued to progress, and two weeks after our discharge, we were ready for a weekend visit at home. Since we were still unable to drive, my dad picked us up. Poor Ken had to recline in the passenger seat, keeping slack in the seat belt to protect his painful incision. Driving over potholes and uneven pavement was painful.

I had to sit between the two girls' booster seats, which was tight and uncomfortable. The discomfort was worth it, and it was so nice to come back to our home, which we hadn't seen since prior to the surgery. It felt weird pulling into our driveway and recalling the state of mind I was in a few weeks earlier when we headed to New York. Now we were home after so much had happened! It was lovely being welcomed home with cards, flowers (although technically not allowed due to infection risk), and multiple gift packages.

We were only home for two days before we needed to get back to the city for Ken's next appointment, but we made the most of it while we were there. Being in the comfort of our home was wonderful. My parents watched the girls at their house around the corner, which was a nice break. Ken and I returned to our pre-child state, taking walks on the beach and then watching movies on the couch.

We were even paid a visit from a local reporter. It happened this way: when we were in New York after the surgery, I had put a few finishing touches on a personal essay I had mostly written prior to the surgery. "A Perfect Match" was a brief love story of Ken and me and the transplant. I submitted it to a local New Age newspaper. They declined to publish it, but I didn't take it too hard. I felt like I couldn't claim to be a writer without having a submission—or a rejected submission. The time and effort I spent working on my piece had brought great value to me. I also had faith it would find a home somewhere else, and our story would be told.

As I was recovering after the surgery, I loved reading all the emotional stories of people's experiences with organ donation on DonateLife.net. I was shocked by the number of people in need of an organ. Their stories were so emotionally driven, and many people had to wait a long time. Fortunately, because I was a match, that wasn't the case for us.

I was very moved by the awareness and work that Donate Life was doing to promote and explain organ donation and how people could get involved. I purchased many items from their online store, including rubber bracelets and pins stating "Donor, "Recipient," "Caretaker," "Donor Family," "Recipient Family," and even the Spanish version, "Donar Vida," to disperse to all the wonderful family and friends who had reached out and lovingly supported us. I also purchased a T-shirt that said 'Lifesaver, Register to be a donor at RegisterMe.org'.

I enjoyed showing my support for Donate Life. To call attention to the need for donors, I wore the shirt and "Donor" pin, and I put a magnet on my car—which unfortunately fell off. I even went so far as to add their banner on the signature portion of my email to spread the word as much as I could. I thought about submitting our story to DonateLife.net, but then I got the idea to contact our local newspaper, *The Southampton Press*, to see if they would be interested in our story. They responded to my email almost immediately and set up a visit with a reporter at our house.

The reporter was lovely and took our picture and contacted me after the interview to clarify a few points. I had told her about my essay, and she asked if she could use some of it to assist her in writing her article. I readily agreed. Although my essay hadn't been published, its message would be heard, and my efforts to increase public awareness of Donate Life would be seen by many readers. To my surprise, the article about Ken and me made the front page of the following week's edition. It did mention Donate Life, and many people told me they had seen the article. I was glad to see our story being told. It all felt worthwhile.

Back in New York, we had the apartment for two more weeks. After this first month, Ken would only need to go to follow-up visits once a week. We made the best of our remaining time in the city. When we had actually lived in Manhattan, our girls were just babies. Now they were old enough to appreciate the things in New York I had always wanted to do with them. We had tea at Alice's Tea Cup on the Upper West Side. I took them to a kids' yoga class at my favorite yoga center where I had done my teacher training, and we found a Rudolf Steiner bookstore that had all sorts of cool Waldorf education books and rare craft items.

In New York, we had play dates with friends I rarely saw anymore, enjoyed frozen yogurt at a wide variety of establishments, and took countless subway rides to find bookstores and new playgrounds. These were simple adventures, things that New York residents take for granted. We loved it. Ken's parents took them to the Statue of Liberty, but Ken and I were not up for such a big undertaking yet. I was so glad they got this glorious experience, and it even inspired Eliza to dress up as the Statue of Liberty for Halloween. The many weeks we spent in New York that summer were certainly difficult and challenging, but we also made the most of them. I felt blessed and grateful that we managed to collect so many wonderful memories.

At the end of August, it was time to return to Hampton Bays. Ken and I were getting much stronger, but we still couldn't lift anything heavier than a jug of milk, so my childhood best friend came to help us pack up. It was the week before Labor Day, and we were anxious to go home and settle in before the kids went back to school.

Memorial Day weekend had been a good representation of our former life. Labor Day weekend brought a new lifestyle with new restrictions. Due to the risk of our incisions softening, or possibly getting infected, Ken and I were no longer able to swim. We could no longer carry beach chairs, coolers, or paddleboards. In fact, we were restricted from lifting anything weighing more than ten pounds. Ken, due to photosensitivity from one of the transplant medications, was not able to spend long periods of time in the sun. There would be no beach volleyball. There was to be no alcohol consumption.

When we were in our twenties and early thirties, I remember being at work in New York City, staring at the clock, anxiously waiting to jump on the subway to Penn Station. Labor Day weekend was the last summer weekend, the last opportunity of the summer to get out to the Hamptons. The trains were always excessively congested. We would race through the sea of people to board the train. It was always standing room only. All of us weekenders eagerly fighting our way to Hampton Bays to make it in time for happy hour and the Friday evening parties.

We were overjoyed to be back in Hampton Bays, but this weekend was going to be considerably different from all the other Labor Day weekends we had celebrated. On Thursday, Ken and I enjoyed an intimate and supportive dinner at a friend's house. We went home early because the next morning, Friday, Ken had a routine post transplant cystoscopy. The procedure was successful and came with some extra fatigue and soreness. An afternoon nap and family beach walk late in the day with the kids was the perfect remedy. Everyone was leaving the beach and heading to restaurants or barbecues. We were going against the grain by just getting to the beach. I always loved getting carried away with the high energy of the weekend, but I was enjoying our new pace. I was grateful that we were healthy and back home in our beautiful beach town. I felt peace and contentment.

That evening, I went to dinner with a friend on Shelter Island, while Ken stayed home to rest. It was nice to be getting out, even if it was in a new modified way. On Saturday morning, I started the day with another beach walk. This time, I enjoyed the solitude of my solo walk contemplating all the changes, when I received a phone call from my mother-in-law. She was experiencing abdominal pain and on her way to the ER—to the hospital where Ken was employed. Thankfully, it didn't end up being serious, however it was upsetting to see her get admitted. My mother-in-law loved few things more than spending Labor Day weekend on the beach with her family. Unfortunately, this year she would not. It was another example of the unusual trends of the weekend. It went on with a Saturday evening BBQ at my mom's house. Sunday continued with the fun of the Hampton Labor Day snapper derby (a fishing contest for the kids) and then out to dinner with Ken's side of the family. My poor mother-in-law was still in the hospital receiving antibiotics, but she insisted we end the summer together with a family dinner at one of our favorite spots on the water. We tried to enjoy ourselves, but all of the changes of the weekend felt heavy.

The light of Monday morning cleared away the heaviness. I had put all of the emotions in perspective and was feeling great. Three months prior, on the Monday of Memorial Day weekend, I had been in tears about all of the upcoming changes the summer would bring and the fear of the unknown. Now, we had made it through the summer, the transplant, and Labor Day weekend. The weekend had its ups and downs, but we persevered! A shift had occurred, and there was an empowering feeling that we had survived—and maybe even thrived.

As I was basking in the gratitude of this empowered shift, I took another walk around my neighborhood. This time, I noticed some abdominal discomfort on my left side. It was strange, but I didn't want to alarm myself, or anyone else, and assumed it was just cramping as a result of my first menstrual cycle since the surgery. I made it home from my walk. Over the next few hours the pain progressed and became extreme. The next thing I knew, I was screaming on the bathroom floor, unable to stand. I needed medical intervention, but I couldn't get in the car. I was paralyzed in pain and fear. I was glad that the girls were at my mom's house and didn't have to witness any of this. I told Ken to call 911. The ambulance showed up quickly, and the paramedics managed to get me on a stretcher and into the ambulance. For the first time in my life, I saw the inside of an ambulance. The pain was so severe, I barely noticed where I was. I begged the EMT, and God, to help me. The EMT administered Dilaudid, a fast-acting pain reliever that helped take the edge off as we headed to the hospital—the same one where my mother-in-law was being treated.

Ken had just received medical clearance to drive again and followed the ambulance in our car. My dad met us at the hospital. I was still in bad shape as they wheeled me into the ER. This was Ken's first time back at the hospital where he worked, as he was on medical leave. He hadn't even gone to visit his mom because he wasn't supposed to be in a high-germ environment. The ER doctors were trying to grasp the situation. It was a bizarre scenario: my severe and mysterious pain, Ken being back in the hospital only one month post kidney transplant, coupled with my mother-in-law admitted in a hospital room upstairs.

There were many cycles of IV opioids. The medication would relieve the pain then wear off and the excruciating pain would return necessitating more medication, only to be repeated. The pain seemed to be coming from my ovary. The ER obstetrician sent me for an ultrasound and CT scan, both of which came back negative. The surgical team, reviewing the CT scan, could see my recent nephrectomy but no other pathology in my abdomen. It was strange to be in a hospital again, and it was even stranger to be experiencing pain worse than the postsurgical pain. The postsurgical pain had been intense and felt foreign, but I understood it. It felt justified. This unknown pain was a lot scarier because it was unclear why I was having it. They admitted me to the hospital and I sent Ken and my dad home. There would be no further intervention, other than continuing to administer pain medication and monitoring me.

There was an available room on the maternity floor, so I was moved up to it around one or two o'clock in the morning. I was still in pain, but the medication was controlling it. It was nice to be on the quiet floor, and I was grateful for the warm maternity nurses who took care of me like a family member. The pain started to subside slightly, and, combined with the exhaustion from the long day, I fell asleep.

When I woke up on Tuesday morning, the pain was completely gone! The surgical team and the OB team cleared me to go home. There was no real explanation for the pain—perhaps intermittent ovarian torsion or a really large ovarian cyst that had ruptured. The surgical team and the OB team were puzzled but happy. This bizarre event was definitely unsettling, still, I was trying to reassure myself with the fact that all my tests had come back normal. By the afternoon, I was back home. I felt tired but fine. I told myself to keep the faith. I told myself my body was healthy.

Nevertheless, with every passing day, I worried. *What if it happened again?* A week later, I traveled to New York City to see the surgeon who had performed my nephrectomy. A few weeks after that, I went to see my midwife to continue my investigation and try to identify what had caused this painful event. I saw multiple medical professionals who all assured me I was in good health. Even Ken's transplant surgeon didn't have any definitive answers, but I felt some comfort when she said, "Hey, the first menstrual cycle after abdominal surgery, you never know".

That helped, and when the next month's period came, I carried around a small bottle of narcotic pain relievers from my kidney surgery. I had never used them because they made me feel dizzy. Having the medication in my bag gave me peace of mind that if the pain came back I would be prepared. Thankfully, it never did, and I never took them.

In spite of my fear that the pain would return, I was undoubtedly in good health. This was not only evidenced by all the test results and the opinions of all the healthcare practitioners that I had seen, but I also began to feel that the universe and God were sending me a message. I felt a sensation of well being move through me. Inspired by this feeling of the presence of a higher power, I made a conscious decision to release the trauma this bizarre scenario had caused. I decided to stop doubting and start accepting. I let go of the fear of the pain coming back and made a conscious decision to bask in the gratitude of being in good health.

The day after I left the hospital was the girls' first day of school. Thankfully, I was better and able to be there to watch Eliza's first day of second grade and Madeleine's first day of kindergarten. The first day of school is always an emotional milestone, but this one was especially so.

Dropping the girls off at school, I noticed the parking lot filled with other families doing the same thing. We were all feeling the energy, excitement, and tears associated with the first day of school. Peconic Community School is home to a loving community of warm people who feel like family. They greeted us with hugs and, in casual conversation, asked how my summer had been. We hadn't seen each other since June and most of them didn't know about the surgery. It was a seemingly simple question, but it startled me. I had been busy over the past few weeks transitioning from New York life, and I just had my bizarre episode two days earlier. Up till now, for me, there was before the surgery and after the surgery, pre op and post op. Now, suddenly, this simple question activated a vivid sense memory causing me to remember the surgery itself, and to relive the day of the transplant. A tear formed in my eye.

Standing in that school parking lot, it all came back to me. I recalled the dark walk up Fort Washington Avenue to the hospital. I was holding Ken's hand. It was five o'clock in the morning. Our backpacks were meticulously packed with cell phone chargers, books, playing cards, underwear and toiletries. We felt like we were going into battle, on vacation, or somewhere in between. As it slowly got lighter, the view of the George Washington Bridge became more visible and revealed the Hudson River and the New Jersey horizon. The coming day was evident only by the increase of light, which also revealed clouds as it began to lightly rain. We increased our pace to avoid the rain. Before we knew it, the walk was over. As we approached Milstein Hospital, it felt like a departure from the outside world, from New York City, and from our former lives. As we walked by the valet stand and entered through the revolving door into the already busy lobby, we encountered employees, patients, and visitors. We approached the desk and handed the security guard our driver's licenses to get our temporary ID badges. The feeling we were doing something big was palpable.

We continued our journey past the security desk and turned into the vast, wide-open atrium of the newly renovated Heart Center. We headed down the long hallway and followed signs to the surgery wing to check in. The luxurious space made us feel like we were in an upscale hotel. The views through the giant floor-to-ceiling windows were majestic. We sat there in the modern, posh waiting room overlooking the Hudson River and watched the morning light fighting through the clouds. It was a wonderful surprise to see my aunt enter the waiting room. We hadn't expected her. My parents would arrive when we got out of surgery. The children were with Ken's parents; all had been taken care of, and it was time.

We were taken back to the bustling, well-lit surgical preparation area. A curtain separated our beds. There were many nurses, technicians, and others coming in and out, taking our vital signs, asking us if we had eaten anything, and giving instructions to change into our hospital gowns and put on our blue surgical elastic head covers. Next came visits from each of our surgeons. They came in separately to say hello and answer any final questions. They marked our abdomens with Sharpies, and then it was time for another emotional goodbye.

The first big farewell for Ken and me was when we were leaving for college. Although we had grown up in the same town, it wasn't until the summer before we left for college that we fell in love and had a proper romantic goodbye. While we were in college in South Carolina and Virginia, the goodbyes kept coming. Both schools were far from our New Jersey homes. With each visit we grew closer, and as our love grew, each goodbye got harder.

After college, there were coast-to-coast goodbyes. Ken would stay in New Jersey, and I would fly to San Francisco, crying most of the way. Then there was going home to separate apartments in Hoboken and New York City. Even a few short months after our wedding, it was goodbye for a month when I went to India.

Yes, we were good at goodbyes, but they were hard, and this one, as we headed to the OR, was the hardest. I had already cried four times, and it wasn't even seven o'clock. As we ripped ourselves apart from our final hug, I started sobbing as I walked away from Ken. All the planning had perfectly fallen into place, and although I felt my spirit guides holding my hands and walking in with me, the tears kept coming.

The double doors opened to a gigantic room filled with stainless steel tables and surgical instruments perfectly lined up and sterilized on blue disposable nonwoven cloths. There were a handful of people in light blue scrubs, shoe coverings, and head covers matching the ones Ken and I were wearing. They were busily preparing for the surgery. The operating table was in the middle of the room, and a step led up to it. Above it, there was a giant light.

The room was cold, but the bed was heated. I climbed onto it and looked around. People were putting IVs in my arms and strapping me down. Breathing deeply and praying to God, I silently recited my mantras: You can do this. You are strong. Right kidney, you can work effectively on your own. Left kidney, it's time to fulfill your divine mission. I repeated the statements over and over while looking at all of the masked faces.

I was surprised when I recognized a pair of eyes.

Ken's surgeon said, "Do you recognize me?"

"Yes," I replied. "You will be here with me?"

"Yes. I stay here until they hand me the kidney, and then I take it to the next room over to Ken."

My eyes filled again, and tears ran down the sides of my head. "Please take good care of him."

She smiled and said, "Of course."

That was my last memory in my original body with my two kidneys still inside.

As I stood there in the school parking lot and looked at the parent who had so innocently and politely asked how my summer was, I wondered how to sum that up.

# CHAPTER 7

# Divine Wake Up

Rebirth: A Spiritual Reawakening after Waking Up from Surgery

I walk into the OR,
My left side marked with an X,
Crying in fear,
But in agreement.
I want to do this.
I wish everyone in the room peace and love and pray that everything
    that goes on in this room will be purposeful, professional, and in my
    highest good.
I see beautiful eyes.
I let go and go to sleep.

I start to return to my body.
Eyes closed, I feel myself coming back to reality.
Although I can't see, my mind starts to process, reminding me of the
    surgery, and I reason I must be in the recovery room.
My eyes want to open, yet are too heavy. A warm feeling comes over me.
A voice whispers in my ear.
It says, "You can do this."
It doesn't feel like a high school sports coach or a fan cheering on an
    athlete,
It's a divine voice,
A divine force, whose tone speaks cosmic wisdom with absolute clarity.

I open my eyes.
The nurse by my bed says, "Take it easy."
That's when I panic.
*Where am I?*
*Did my husband get out of surgery?*
*I can't move. What is that pain?*

I see the nurse's gentle face and feel the divine force again.
I take a deep breath and feel calmer.
"Can I see my mom?"
He nods.
My family is outside and can come in soon.
I fall back to sleep.

One month later, here I sit,
At home, my husband by my side.
We are thriving. It is done.
We are on the other side.
Goodbye, left kidney; you have served me well,
Please continue your divine work. Keep my husband alive.
Thank you, right kidney, for stepping up and working solo. I know you can.
And thank you, God. I am reborn.

\*\*\*

"Good news," my recovery room nurse states. "Your bed upstairs is ready, and you are being transferred out of recovery."

I am too drowsy for the news to faze me one way or the other. My more immediate concern is the pain, which is awakening slowly like a bear from hibernation. It's raw, primitive, and hungry. I recognize the feeling because it occurred three hours earlier when the previous dose of Dilaudid, a strong narcotic pain reliever, wore off.

Still new to all this, I start to squirm and panic, but the new dose puts me back into a comfortably numb state. I fall back to sleep, and the cycle continues. It's a pattern I repeat many times. I wake up. I request the new dose. I tell the nurse how tired I feel. He comfortingly advises me to keep sleeping. He uses the analogy that it's like sleeping off a hangover. Sleep will help clear my body of the anesthesia used during the surgery. Every time I fall asleep and wake up again, I never know how long it's been. Time has no relevance, and most sleep episodes end with bizarre dreams that frantically wake me up.

"How about switching to Percocet?" the nurse suggests. "It lasts longer."

I reluctantly agree. The postsurgical pain is so foreign yet very specific. It seems justified, but it scares me. Still, I have faith it will eventually lose its raw hunger.

The nurse brings the Percocet. I ask how my husband is. I haven't seen him since our presurgical goodbye.

The nurse tells me he is doing well.

The transport stretcher arrives to wheel me upstairs. My head starts to feel incredibly light.

"When do I get to see him?"

The transport technician offers to wheel me by him on our way up.

Thankful wouldn't begin to describe my gratitude. I am in a supine position, unable to move, and my head starts to spin as the bed moves. We wheel past a few other stretchers, and that's when I catch a glimpse of him behind a curtain. He sees me too.

"Babe!" he yells. His recovery bed is elevated at forty-five degrees. He looks happy to see me, but he has an artificial and chemical look on his face.

I see a big plastic box on an IV pole. "Are you okay?" I ask, tears in my eyes.

"Yes, I'm okay."

I breathe the biggest sigh of relief of my life.

"Are you in pain?"

I realize that the plastic box is a PCA pump. I used to see them when I worked as a physical therapist with post surgical patients. Patient-controlled analgesia (PCA) pumps supply opioid, pain controlling, drugs into a patient's IV. I wonder why he has the pump. My foggy and delayed mental processing answers my thought, and I shudder at the realization, indicated by the PCA pump, of the severity of pain he is experiencing.

I have known my husband for more than twenty-five years. In that time, despite the years of kidney failure, medications, and surgical procedures, I have rarely ever heard him complain of pain or discomfort. He is usually full of energy. Now he is recovering from major surgery and on a continuous pump to medicate the excruciating pain he is in. I feel a knot in my stomach and become aware of my lightheadedness, which is quickly evolving into nausea.

In spite of the queasiness, I try to capture this moment. Ken's surgical cap is covering his head, and his dark eyes are glassy. His smile is huge, and although I know it is chemically enhanced, I can feel the sincerity in it. I don't want to leave, but I begin to feel like I am going to vomit. The transport technician and I resume our journey up to my new unit. Ken stays in the recovery unit. It's goodbye again. This time, there are no tears; the nausea is the dominant force.

The hallways, as I quickly pass by on the moving stretcher, have a faint familiarity. My head continues to spin. The nausea is now severe. I am comforted by memories of when I was a newly graduated physical therapist, my professional career ahead of me. I remember the feeling of walking down these very same halls with pride, knowing that my very first PT job was working at such a highly respected medical institution. It was also my first job in New York City. Living and working there felt like the Frank Sinatra lyric; I had made it there—and I could make it anywhere. As a new employee, I had felt small, inexperienced, and in over my head. However, deep down, I also felt incredibly accomplished and proud. Now I am a patient in the same place where all those memories occurred. Remembering all this is a good distraction and probably the only thing that prevents me from throwing up all over myself as we enter the giant patient elevator.

Looking at the round-lit button indicating nine on the elevator panel, I ask the transport technician which unit we are going to. She states that we are going up to the McKeen Pavilion.

I am wonderfully shocked. When I had been a new employee in this very hospital, our department occasionally received PT orders for patients in the McKeen Pavilion: the hospital's VIP unit. Usually only the more experienced therapists were allowed to perform evaluations and treatments for the patients on this luxurious floor. The McKeen Pavilion provides menus to its patients and serves a variety of gourmet food. It even distributes a daily newspaper (like a hotel). It also has an elegant atrium with a grand piano, a waterfall, and afternoon tea. Bill Clinton stayed here after his cardiac procedure.

It turns out that organ donors also stay in the McKeen Pavilion, and even though I have arrived in a nauseous state, a small wave of happiness comes over me. This unit is much quieter and calmer than the recovery unit I have just come from. As I enter, the nurses give me a round of applause. I look confused. They justify their applause by saying, "You saved a life today".

I wasn't expecting the praise. With all that had gone on that day, it was hard to receive such a warm welcome. I hardly felt (or looked) like a hero. Nobility never crossed my mind in the transplant decision-making process. It was more a feeling of necessity and inevitability mixed with the hardship of fitting this complicated scenario into our lives, careers, schedules and thinking about how it would affect the kids. There was also gratitude for the miracle that I was a match, and that Ken would not have to wait on a list. Not to mention being thankful for the modern medical advances that made a kidney transplant possible. Ken's love and support had been the foundation I built my life on. I never thought twice about being a donor. Therefore, being praised for virtue didn't seem accurate.

Nevertheless, as I enter the welcoming luxury of the McKeen Pavilion, I am grateful for the acknowledgment, for the applause, and for the warm comments about my heroism. At the same time, the nausea and lightheadedness haven't gone away, and are slowly morphing into agitation. The nurse offers me medication for the nausea, but knowing that it was Percocet that made me nauseous in the first place, I decline. What I need is sleep. Sleep is the remedy for how I am feeling.

The nurses and the transport technician lift me from my temporary stretcher to my more permanent hospital bed. Relieved, I close my eyes and go right back to sleep. A little later, I wake up frantically again, from more bizarre dreams. When I come to, I realize it is evening. The nausea has subsided. The nurse comes in and tells me Ken is still in the recovery unit. I am disappointed, but the good news is that he is doing well—and I focus on my next order of business: getting out of bed.

The surgery was at seven o'clock this morning. It is now ten o'clock at night. After such a long day, I long to assess the status of my mobility. I haven't moved in what feels like forever. When I worked these floors as a PT, my job was to get people out of bed regardless of the condition they were in or what they had been through.

I peel away the covers and examine the bandages on my body. There are tubes and lines coming out of me. I had gone to sleep with my body intact. It is strange and disorienting seeing my abdomen with three small, bandaged scope holes and a larger incision just above my pubic region from which the kidney was harvested. I have never had surgery before.

In order to roll onto my side and sit up on the edge of the bed, the nurse and I move the Foley catheter line and associated urine bag aside and organize my IV lines. The roll to my right side is painful, but I am determined to continue. Sitting at the edge of the bed, I am slightly lightheaded. Just as I had done with my own patients many times when getting them out of bed after their surgeries, I instruct myself to take some deep breaths.

When I stand up, I feel the force of gravity and an intense pressure on my lower incision. I feel the weight of my internal organs and fluids pressing on it. It feels like it will burst open. To my pleasant surprise, my feet feel stable and can bear my body weight. I stand up straighter with the help of the nurse. I walk out of my room and down the hall. I look out the window at the Hudson River. I turn around and go back to my room. It is only fifteen hours after my surgery, and I am satisfied with the short walk. I feel accomplished. I go back to bed and back to sleep.

In the middle of the night, the nursing shift changes. A new warm face wakes me while taking my vital signs and administering the heparin (blood-thinning) shot that I dread. She introduces herself and says she has a message for me. Ken has made it up from recovery and is in the unit adjacent to mine. The message is, ' He loves you'. Tears come to my eyes. I will be seeing him in the morning. I am so excited.

On Thursday morning, my first order of business is walking to Ken's room. The transplant unit is on the ninth floor, a little more than 150 feet away. My nurse escorts me. I am eager, but slow moving, as I venture down the hallway.

When I get to the door of Ken's room, I see a cart with masks and specialized equipment for visitors to wear in order to avoid bringing germs into the room. I walk in and see 'my rock' in his hospital bed. He looks disheveled, tired and uncomfortable, but I am so grateful to see him. My nurse assists me into a bedside chair and leaves to let us visit.

I ask him how he is feeling, and he says, "Okay, but in pain and uncomfortable." He can't get up yet because he is still connected to his PCA pump and a long infusion of IV immunosuppressive medication.

Although this is only the second time on my feet, my PT instincts kick in. I raise myself up to stand at the side of Ken's bed, and I say, "If you can't get out of bed and walk, let's at least sit you at the edge of the bed."

He is reluctant, but I am determined to see him move and hopefully get him into a more comfortable position. I organize the many lines and tubes coming out of him and instruct him to roll onto his side, get his legs off the edge, and sit up.

Just by sitting up, he already looks so much better.

I tell him to pump his ankles up and down. While he is doing this, I rearrange his bedding and the Chuck pad on top of the fitted sheet so it won't be wrinkled under him when he lies back down.

After he has been sitting for a while, I say, "Let's try to stand. It felt so liberating when I stood up last night. If you feel weak, you can sit right back down."

He stands up, and he resembles my husband again—not some disheveled, sick patient. I breathe another giant sigh of relief. After standing a moment or two, he sits back down and gets back into bed.

I feel so much satisfaction. It is post-op day one, and Ken and I have both been up on our feet. I sit with him a bit longer and then go back to my room. This reunion has been glorious, but I know I need to pace myself. Hospital days are long. Healing requires rest.

It has already been an eventful morning, but it is still early; visiting hours will be starting soon. My parents will arrive first, and after that, my in-laws will be coming by with the children. I am excited and eager to see them all.

I rest, and even manage to sleep for a while. When I wake up, I put on the new nightgown and matching robe my sister bought me for the surgery. I also take my pain medication. That's when I realize how hungry I am starting to feel. I haven't eaten anything, other than some Jell-O and broth, since the night before the surgery.

The doctors and nurses clear me to have lunch. The dietary employee arrives and hands me a menu. I am starving, but also overwhelmed by the wide selection of food; it all sounds delicious. I finally make my selection: tomato soup and a grilled cheese sandwich. I am overjoyed when it arrives and is served to me. I eat every bite. I'm looking forward to seeing my family.

When visiting hours begin, I have a wonderful visit with my parents. Then my in-laws arrive with the children. I'm so happy to see them. I have been especially eager to see our two girls, Eliza and Maddy. I have wondered how they would react seeing Ken and me as hospital patients. I make it a point to show them my incisions so they understand why they can't sit on my lap and why I am not allowed to pick them up. I let them play with my incentive spirometer (a plastic breathing apparatus designed to help take deep breaths and prevent pneumonia). Then we sit in the beautiful atrium and have afternoon tea. Although I love our time together, I quickly hit a wall and need everyone to leave.

The rest of the afternoon and evening brings an emotional wave of tears. This feels similar to the episode I experienced after Memorial Day. Lots of emotions have built up and it all needs to come out. So much has happened. So much is still happening. My copious tears seem more than justified but also feel painful, like broken shards of glass, as they come out.

I am grateful we have made it through the operations, but it is hard to feel lighthearted. I need to clear the darkness first. The pain I am experiencing is rough. Every time my abdominal muscles engage against my incision, there is a sharp pain. Every time I stand, gravity creates a strong pressure against my lower incision. It seems I have taken for granted how my thick skin tightly contains my insides. My new incision doesn't seem like it is up to the task of holding it all in. The intense pressure is excruciating. I tell myself it will subside as I stand longer, that I just need time to adjust to this new feeling. I feel guilty about making such a big deal of all this. Ken's incision is much bigger than mine, and seeing him squirming in pain has made my empathic self feel a double edged sword of shame and self-pity.

I cry inconsolably the whole day. I can't help myself. The tears keep coming. Everyone who comes to see me—nurses, doctors, family and friends—are witnesses to my sobbing. As word about my heavy emotions is spreading among the transplant team, one of the doctors takes it upon himself to talk to Ken.

Ken's nephrologist asks him if my sadness is a result of feeling a sense of loss from giving my kidney. Ken and I both assure everyone it isn't that. I'm okay—just very emotional about everything that is going on. As an empath, someone who is highly sensitive when it comes to emotions, I feel everything that happens to me very deeply, and while others are able to adjust in difficult emotional situations, I simply cannot. The tears just keep coming. Since the grieving is so intense, I even ask for pastoral services to come visit me.

Ken and I keep getting a plethora of calls, texts, and visitors checking up on us. People keep saying how strong and brave we are. I read the messages and listen to the comments with tears streaming down my face. I, for one, do not feel an ounce of strength or bravery.

I am able to find comfort in the lyrics to a song I love by Jana Stanfield: "You don't have to feel brave to be brave. I don't have to feel strong to be strong." Those words save me, and as the afternoon turns into evening and becomes the next morning, post-op day two, I realize the crying is cleansing out all the old fears and painful emotions, making way for the new light that is on its way in.

On Friday morning, I am looking out at the sun rising on the Hudson River; I feel my emotional episode subsiding. All the crying has felt like a cleansing, a closure, a moving away from the pain of my former life, the pain from the fear leading up to the surgery, the pain from walking into the OR, and the pain from two very intense days in recovery. This emotional outpouring of the last few days has been my way of letting go and surrendering.

I have been grieving my perception of the loss of our life before the surgery. After thirty-seven years, I had come to love everything about my life: the fun-filled days in high school and college, traveling to San Francisco, my twenties in New York City, weekend trips to the Hamptons, our wedding in Montauk, and my children being born. So much fear of the transplant was saying goodbye to my old life, which contained all the good times and not so good times I was clinging too.

I was so grateful for the life Ken and I had built together, and I was scared of what our future would bring. Ken would have to be on immunosuppressive therapy for the rest of his life, and I feared how our life would change as a result. The list of restrictions was long—no alcohol for three months, no public transportation, no lifting, no beach volleyball or swimming—and the list went on. Of course, Ken's health was more important than any of those things, and we did eventually find a way to come to terms with each and every one of them. However, it all hit me at once: starting a new life, what that meant, and sorting it all out.

And so, I surrendered to all that emotion and cried it all out, which helped clear it all away. The beauty of a new day came, and the light of Friday morning brought relief along with the beautiful epiphany that Ken and I had survived the surgery. We were in one of the best hospitals in the world, we had a wonderful network of family and friends, and we still had each other! As long as we had that, we could make a new life going forward, and that is exactly what we did!

This obstacle became an opportunity, and our new life was different and eventually became better than ever. By Friday morning rounds, I told the transplant team I was ready to go home. I was at least ready to go the four blocks to the apartment we would be staying in for the month. I had another delicious gourmet lunch and then spent the afternoon preparing for my discharge. I even managed to take a shower, and when my surgeon came in to see me one last time, he commented about how well I looked and made one last comment about how brave I was.

A few final tears came, and then my dear friend, and designated caregiver, came to escort me home. The nurse gave me my final discharge instructions, and another transport technician picked me up. This time, I would be transported in a wheelchair. She wheeled me to Ken's room, and I said goodbye to him. It was sad to part again. I was comforted by the team saying if all of the insurance logistics were in order and he could leave with all the necessary medication, there was a good chance Ken would be discharged the next day.

The transporter wheeled me through the lobby and to the entrance. I stood up and slowly walked the four blocks down Fort Washington Avenue. I felt like a completely different person. Although I walked slowly, I felt empowered. I had done it; I had donated my kidney to my husband!

Two months later, right on schedule, Ken went back to work at our local hospital as the director of hospital medicine. I returned to my position as full-time mom, aspiring writer, occasional physical therapist, and home manager, among other things. All in all, it was a fairly smooth transition, and life was back on track. I felt blessed that we survived the transplant and were closer than ever. Life was good.

While Ken and I were healing, I loved the snail's pace life we were leading. Returning to the fast-paced life we led prior to the transplant was hard. Everything had been on hold, but Ken going back to work meant facing a lot of those items that were waiting. Of course, everyone was very understanding, and we made great efforts to ease back in and not dive in headfirst.

I slowly started picking up the pace as we resumed our fall routines: chaperoning school field trips, Halloween preparations, and trips to local farms to pick pumpkins and apples. Our family even started to resume weekend trips to Massachusetts to visit family and friends and to Montauk to celebrate birthdays. The doctors eased Ken's restrictions regarding crowded places. We went to Atlantic City for the weekend and to a Jets game in New Jersey—where we got to go on the field!

Initially, I could feel the tension in my neck and shoulders as I started to pick up the pace—working around the house, grocery shopping, cooking, and preparing lunches—but I was determined to pace myself. So much had happened, and returning to my writing gave me the perfect vehicle to reflect on what it all meant. I felt like I had a new lease on life. I was moving in a new direction.

There was so much to write about, but I took my time through the rest of the fall and winter. As Ken and I continued to recover, I was observing how this new life was unfolding. I loved my old life, but in this new one—starting with my spiritual rebirth—I felt born into a new body that was more self-aware, intuitive, lighter (literally without a kidney) and better than ever. From this new vantage point, I started to notice some interesting new qualities emerging in Ken.

I had known Ken since middle school. He was always smart, witty, pragmatic, and very masculine with his love of football and other 'dude' things. However, as the winter gave way to spring, I began to see some of my female energies manifesting in him. Talking to other donors and recipients, I learned that they too shared this experience. Upon further research, I discovered the concept of *cellular memory*: the hypothesis that the body is capable of storing memories and personality traits in cells and organs other than the brain. The work in this area is limited, but it is believed that when one receives an organ from another, they can experience the memories and personality traits of the donor.

Clearly, this was not mentioned during any of our transplant preparations. This more esoteric, mind-body work has been mentioned by Deepak Chopra but not in the traditional medical establishment, to no surprise. I also read a memoir by Claire Sylvia, a recipient of a double lung and heart transplant. *A Change of Heart* discusses her experiences after the transplant. In her book, she tells of dreams she had about her donor, including his name, despite none of his information being available to her before or after the transplant. She also experienced some aspects of his personality, and even more surprisingly, some of his food preferences.

In the early spring, six or seven months after the transplant, I saw Ken pick up a basket of wool roving and tools used to needle felt—a crafting technique done in Waldorf schools—and he proceeded to make a felted dolphin. It was amazing! I had tried to pick up this art and teach it to the kids, but I rarely got anywhere with it. Before my eyes, I saw Ken making different animals—one after the other—as if he had been doing it for years! We gave them away as gifts to new babies and cousins, and it was fun to see the look of surprise on people's faces when they said, "Ken, you made this?"

Some other examples were not as obvious to others—more sensitivity and intuition—but they were quite obvious to me. We felt closer than ever, and seeing this new creative energy in him, which felt like it came from me, was magical. After all the creative recovery I had experienced in the past year, seeing it reflected in Ken, and in my new life, felt like another heartwarming miracle.

# CHAPTER 8

# Sobriety, God, and More Recovery

The first Alcoholics Anonymous (AA) meeting I attended was when I was in college at the University of South Carolina. I was enjoying the typical freshman experience of partying mixed with a little bit of studying. At that time, USC had a small strip of bars that underage college kids like me could get into. Depending on the night, we would either sneak in through the back door or rush in with a group through the front door past the rare bouncer who was checking IDs. We even got friendly with the right staff members who would simply escort us in. It was risky, but also a college freshman's dream to actually drink at a bar as opposed to consuming stale keg beer at the various run-down locations where fraternities would host parties.

The bubble burst when a friend and I were busted for underage drinking by an undercover cop at one of the bars. I was written a summons to appear in court, and my friend was arrested—I suppose because she appeared drunker than I did. Prior to this event, I had very few run-ins with the law, other than a traffic ticket and high school parties the cops would break up. I was therefore very shaken up by the incident, and picking up my friend from the Columbia Detention Center the next day was quite a contrast to our carefree freshman glory days.

Our freshman partying days were further interrupted by a court order that required us, as part of our pretrial intervention, to attend an Alcoholics Anonymous meeting as well as an alcohol education class. This would prevent the offense from appearing on our permanent records. It was probably then that the thought crossed my mind that maybe I was drinking too much, but it was confusing to decipher, because in the 1990s, binge drinking was rampant. Everyone I was around was drinking just as much—if not way more—than I was. My friends and I would take road trips to visit friends at Emory University, the University of Georgia, and the College of William and Mary, where our friends reported similar experiences at their colleges and universities. Since everyone was doing it, I chalked it all up to the times we were living in, those crazy college drinking days, and I didn't give it much thought after that.

It wasn't until the age of thirty-six, some eighteen years later, that I attended my second AA meeting. I had gone to my local yoga studio intending to attend an eight o'clock class. When I got there, I realized I had misread the schedule. Instead of a yoga class, there was a recovery support group meeting. I was surprised. I had not realized that those types of meetings even occurred at the yoga studio.

A member from the group asked me to stay, but I told her I had come by accident and had intended to go to a yoga class. I went home and thought about the occurrence for several days. Had it been an accident, or was it, in truth, a moment of synchronicity? Giving it some thought, I had to admit it hadn't really felt like an accident. I had walked into an AA meeting. If I was being honest with myself, the idea of synchronicity felt nice, but the next logical thought, the urge to go back, felt uncomfortable. *Why would I want to go back? I don't have a problem, do I?*

Uncomfortable, but feeling a sense of inner soul duty, the next week I went back to the meeting. I sat down on the floor in a circle with the other group members and followed the others' lead. The members of the group shared one by one, going around the circle, bravely acknowledging the various addictions they were facing.

When it was my turn, I stated I was experiencing some troubles, but I wasn't sure if they were alcohol related. It was the summer before the transplant. My kids were four and six, and we were comfortably settled in Hampton Bays. I had returned from Africa a few months prior, and life was good. However, for such a blessed life, I felt like I was battling negative mind chatter more than the average person.

I experienced emotional roller coasters, up one day and down the next, but would attribute it to not going to yoga or not meditating enough or the normal stresses of everyday life and parenting. Although I wasn't a college

113

party girl anymore and had evolved into a responsible mother, I enjoyed blowing off some steam on the weekends or when someone was available to watch the kids, Ken and I would go out and meet friends for drinks. *Yes, I consumed alcohol. But that was normal, wasn't it? That didn't mean I had a problem with alcohol, right?*

As I sat there and contemplated that question, I listened to the other members of the group share. I was very moved by the vulnerability of their stories. I found the acknowledgment of their struggles and their surrender very refreshing. It felt like such a safe space in which to open up. I had always found social situations, with the pressure to engage in small talk and superficial conversation, challenging. There is so much substance deep down within all of us, yet we hide it. I suppose we don't want to reveal our darkness, but that darkness is inside of us. By hiding it and denying our struggles, we miss an opportunity for transformation. In day-to-day life around my children, I keep conversation light and focused on the present moment in an attempt to try and filter out a lot of the complex adult world. At adult parties where people are drinking, the conversation can also feel a bit artificial. By contrast, in this supportive group, I experienced a kind of deep sharing I hadn't fully realized I was longing for.

I really enjoyed the meeting at the yoga studio, nevertheless, I didn't go back. Although I had a profound experience, I was not ready for recovery work yet. However, I did want to face some of the uncomfortable feelings that came up, and I did start to see a therapist whose name I fortuitously got at that meeting. I hadn't been to therapy since my grad school days. I wasn't ready to stop drinking entirely, but I was ready to dig and explore the discomfort that came up around the issue. I started seeing the therapist, Lois, regularly for the next year. It was an incredibly valuable experience. We worked together, and the result was a lot of deep healing, with me gaining a better understanding, not only of myself and my relationships, but also an understanding of the underlying patterns that I too often soothed with alcohol.

I was a very loved child. Even so, I went on to become a somewhat confused adolescent. In high school, college, and living in major cities, alcohol became a big part of my life. There was a seed planted in the back of my mind, something problematic. Yes, I was accepted into college, passed my exams and earned a doctorate in physical therapy. I had read and listened to many people's stories of hitting rock bottom and then entering recovery. Those stories affected me, yet I was landing good jobs and had strong relationships and didn't feel like drinking was interfering in my life. Although I had all of that evidence, I remained unconvinced.

Even though I didn't think I had a problem, I struggled with the issue of my drinking for years, and I remained conflicted until I finally began to realize it wasn't the amount or frequency of my drinking, instead it was the reason *why* I was drinking that was upsetting me. I was drinking to fill a void, a void I somehow knew was present but was too scared to face. When I was in my younger days, coming of age and maturing into myself, drinking was an easy and fun way of filling that void. I didn't quite understand, or accept yet, that I was a more introverted individual who wanted to be more lighthearted and fun. Starting to experiment with alcohol in high school, and suddenly being at parties, made it easier to open up and laugh at all my serious thoughts. I never felt normal as an adolescent or high school student, but drinking made me feel like everyone else. It would temporarily take me out of my thoughts—at least as far as I could remember—and numb my inadequate feelings of feeling different.

Before I knew it, I was being invited to high school parties and hanging out with people I didn't have the courage to talk to when I was sober. I would experience both ends of the spectrum: numbing out and then a vengeance of emotional thoughts at the end of the night or the next morning. The result would be tears or scribbling overdramatically in my journals about being different and no one understanding me.

Then it was off to college and leaving home for the first time. In this new stage of life and new social setting, I was thankful alcohol was there to numb the social anxieties of meeting all these new people. It definitely opened social doors. Numbing my discomforts didn't exactly feel right, but everyone else seemed to be doing it too. I disregarded those thoughts and joined the party.

I always felt I was on a serious quest to find myself. I never thought alcohol would lead the way, but being a lighthearted party girl was a nice break from my serious self. I realize now what I really longed for was to be out experiencing the world. Alcohol was so socially acceptable and readily available. It eased my social anxiety and got me out to exciting places—from underground bars in the Castro in San Francisco to dive bars on the Lower East Side in New York City. I found these edgy environments liberating. Like a social anthropologist, I was fascinated by all the people living lives I could have never even imagined living in the conservative New Jersey suburbs. In those years, I thought drinking was my ticket to getting out and seeing the world. Thankfully, I now know I can still see the sights, experience the eccentricities, and engage in the adventure without the need for alcohol.

Alcohol consumption was obviously paused while I was pregnant. Any pregnant woman will tell you that parties and social situations are brutal. My tool of social grace (or so I thought) was gone, and my typical weekend social life drastically changed. I would show up to a party determined that being pregnant wouldn't change me and go home an hour later. The crowded pushing of the bar would agitate me, but I had hardly noticed it before. Social scenes that I couldn't easily escape—family functions and holidays—were also harder to manage. They became associated with alcohol consumption. I would get annoyed seeing everyone so loose and having fun drinking while I was restricted. When I was a kid, I could be at a party without drinking, but my new normal made it hard to be at a party without drinking. Being stuck at a party and being unable to drink because I was pregnant made me feel like a victim.

After giving birth, alcohol consumption moved to the back of my mind. I was recovering from the birth and bonding with my new baby. I loved breastfeeding and did not want to corrupt my liquid gold. Once my baby was a few months old, I got into a groove. I was able to enjoy a glass of Guinness, which they say is good for breastfeeding. By the time my baby was a year old and starting on solids, although I was still breastfeeding, I was able to find small windows to catch a buzz here and there. My tolerance was so low that two glasses of wine felt euphoric after such a big change in my drinking patterns. These fun little bouts would mostly occur during daytime get-togethers with family and friends. Nighttime was for breastfeeding and co-sleeping.

A year and a half after giving birth, I became pregnant again. Abstaining from drinking was even harder this time around. Being pregnant and running after a two-year-old with no glass of wine at the end of the day was brutal! After my second birth, and breastfeeding for a little more than a year, I slowly started to return to my old friend who was there loyally waiting for me. As a mom of two young children, drinking seemed more than justified. *After all the hard work of caring for kids all day—feeding them, playing with them, bathing them, and getting them to bed—didn't I deserve a reward of a glass of wine, a refreshing beer, or a stiff vodka martini with olives?*

I can see more clearly now. As I was raising my babies, I was also healing my inner child. I dove headfirst into attachment parenting, breastfeeding, co-sleeping, mindful discipline, and limited screen time. It nurtured my children and me. Drinking was my subconscious rebellion to the parenting and inner child work I was doing. I didn't realize any of this at the time. Drinking soothed the wounds, rewarded my hard work, and helped blow off my frustrations. I am happy to say that I did eventually find healthier coping methods.

As my kids got older, there were no drinking limitations from breastfeeding. The kids were sleeping through the night and staying with babysitters and having overnights with grandparents. My outings away from the kids felt like celebrations of freedom—and what better way to celebrate than with a glass of prosecco or a glass of rosé. My drinking habits had evolved from high school keg stands and college funneling days. I rarely stayed out till two o'clock like in those younger days, and on the whole, I consumed way less alcohol. Even though I enjoyed the new sophistication of my drinking, the reasons hadn't changed.

As I saw partying buddies get older and decrease their drinking, they would warn about how much harder the hangovers hit. I never really believed it. I could have a few drinks, and the next morning's headaches could easily be eliminated with a workout or some Tylenol. When I was younger, I could be hungover all day on Sunday and watch movies on the couch and order pizza. I felt a lot of darkness on those days, but the pizza or brunch with Bloody Marys would usually counteract it. By Monday or Tuesday, I would feel like myself again—whatever that meant.

As I was getting older, I started to see why that lifestyle was falling out of favor. The days after were hazy fogs, and I was unable to execute the many tasks I normally did as a mom. My babies didn't really notice, but as my children were getting older, I was wondering what kind of example I was setting. The kids had no idea why Mom was so tired on Sundays. The physical discomfort came with the even worse guilty and destructive thoughts. The physical pain of the hangover combined with the guilty feelings about the night before was torture. I was completely misrepresenting myself, and it began to dawn on me that I was undoing all the transformational work that was meant to uplift me, not to mention negating my hard work to maintain my weight loss.

I stopped drinking the week before the transplant after having a single glass of wine at a gathering. Later that night, I engaged in a mental battle of destructive thoughts. The next day, it was so clear. I was dealing with a big life situation and felt strong mentally and capable physically except when I was drinking. I decided I didn't need the interference, and I figured a sober week before surgery would also be in my best interests health wise.

After the transplant, Ken was advised not to consume any alcohol for three months while he was recovering and adjusting to his immunosuppressive medication regimen. Ken was my favorite of my many drinking buddies, and I told him we would do it together. When the three months were up, the doctors told Ken he could have one drink at a sitting. He was happy and satisfied to enjoy a nice craft beer at a party or dinner.

I, on the other hand, was not ready to go back to drinking, not even one drink at night. The three months of no drinking after the surgery affected me differently than either of my pregnancy abstinence experiences. This time, I was not chomping at the bit to get back to the old drinking routine. I had had a transformative experience. *I had given one of my kidneys to Ken.* I was feeling a newfound clarity. For a while I used having the surgery, and giving Ken my kidney, as my excuse for why I was sober, but it was more than that. The truth was, my head was clearer and life was way better. I could hear the divine applause and that felt like something I wanted to keep hearing.

As Ken and I began to re-engage with our social life, I feared facing the many events in which drinking played a big part. There were so many circumstances: having a glass of Rosé after the beach at our favorite restaurant on the water, Jets games (whether we watched them at home or a friend's house), holidays, cocktail parties, catching up with friends over a drink, and so many more scenarios. Could I get through all of these events without having a drink? As they say in AA, one day at a time.

As each event came up, I would deeply ask myself and then meditate on if or why I wanted to go. Drinking was no longer a motivating factor.

I started to identify the other reasons why going to an event would bring me joy: seeing and connecting with family and friends, going out for a nice meal and not having to cook, being there for my children, the fun of getting out, enjoying the ambience of the event and the music.

I still enjoyed going out, but I started going out much less. It became quality over quantity. My mind-set and intention had shifted. Instead of rushing to the bar, I began to take in the vibe, the atmosphere. When a situation didn't feel right, I would simply decline or show up and leave early. To my surprise, it was easier than I thought.

My third AA meeting was Labor Day weekend, a month after the surgery. Since I wasn't going to be drinking that weekend, I asked a friend if I could join him at a meeting. I was slowly realizing that I wanted to spend the second half of my life sober. Still, I wasn't ready to fully commit or announce my sobriety. Nor was I willing to refer to myself as an alcoholic, but the supportive atmosphere, and being around people who had made this huge commitment, inspired me and showed me that it could be done.

In the meeting, people from all walks of life and various ethnicities and socioeconomic backgrounds were leading sober lives, working together and supporting each other. The various participants would stand up and say how long they had been sober, which varied from a few days to many years. I found it fascinating that people who were sober for decades were still doing the work every day and going to meetings. Regardless of how long they had been in the program, and been struggling to stay sober, they seemed happy with their decisions. I even saw people I knew from the community; I had no idea they were sober and participated in this work.

The meeting really felt like my first one. It was the first time I was there voluntarily. I had my own day count; I had not had a drink in 30 days. I saw the signs with the twelve steps, and I really listened and took it all in. The timing felt right. At AA meetings, there is a lot of mention of the word *God*. I was still fully engaged in *A Course in Miracles,* and being on the other side of the transplant, I definitely felt like I had experienced a miracle. When I received the book from a friend in my 'old life' and started reading it, I worked through my resistance with the word *God,* and our relationship evolved to being acquaintances. Now I was beginning a new life. I was not drinking. After my divine wake-up, I felt my relationship with God evolve even further. I started to genuinely feel the presence of God in my life. It felt as though we were one.

I went to a few more AA meetings, and the sharing of personal stories and devotion to a higher power were refreshingly authentic. I love formal opportunities for sharing, which allow people to open up and be honest and vulnerable. It felt similar to my experience at the Basic Training workshops. Regardless of who we are or our backgrounds, we all have struggles. These opportunities can be painful and uncomfortable but also liberating and allow for healing and transformation when you let it out. After sharing their stories, participants admitted that they were facing a force that was stronger than they were. Rather than resist it, they surrendered to it and asked for help. It was beautiful. The goal wasn't just to stop drinking; it was to evolve spiritually. I respected the process, the acknowledgment of the struggles we face, and then the relief that comes when you "let go and let God." I found it all tremendously inspiring and liked being surrounded by the people doing the work.

It took time to realize it was compulsive behavior that I struggled with, and the term *alcoholic* did not fit my situation. This was not denial. I was willing to admit to heavy drinking, attend the meetings and abstain from drinking. Despite all my fears of what a life without drinking would look like, I was shocked and pleasantly surprised to discover my life was actually better. Sobriety from alcohol was definitely healing me. I had never felt clearer, and I wanted to make a lifelong commitment to it. Nevertheless, I could accept many labels—mother, writer, physical therapist, yogi, free spirit, or even hippie—but *alcoholic* was one shoe that still didn't fit.

A label that does fit me like a glove is empath. I am a highly sensitive person. Judith Orloff's *The Empath's Survival Guide* explains that empaths have an extremely sensitive neurological system and don't have the same filters as others to block out stimulation; therefore, they get easily overstimulated. The book has a whole chapter on "Empaths and Addiction." Orloff, a psychiatrist and an empath, states, "Empaths commonly self-medicate the discomfort of being overstimulated by turning to alcohol, drugs, sex, food, gambling, shopping, and other addictions."

Empaths get overwhelmed and feel too much. If they do not know how to manage the sensory overload, they numb themselves to shut off their thoughts and feelings. Reading this was huge for me, and self-awareness can be so liberating. It had always been so hard, especially in social situations, to manage consumption of alcohol—and food too. Of course, I didn't realize any of this until I stopped drinking.

Being in social situations, I would feel the energies of those around me and an inner chaos would begin to erupt. Some call this social anxiety. Going to parties and not drinking, I began to see how these feelings unfolded and to understand why it was that I had always rushed to grab a drink. At home during the day, while the kids were at school, I noticed that I could manage more easily. The problems came after school, when attending to school activities, caring for the kids, preparing dinner, bath and bedtime, all contributed to my feeling extremely over stimulated and fatigued to the point of agitation. I am certainly not the only mother who has felt exhausted by the end of the day, but my sensitivity to the feelings of exhaustion were definitely the hardest times to face without a drink—or binge on whatever food I could get my hands on.

It became clear that I had always been an empath. Deep down I think I knew this, yet with years of drinking and numbing, the clarity and extent was lacking. I am so grateful I came across this book and couldn't believe it took me thirty-eight years to realize all of this.

In her book, Orloff offers alternatives to self-medicating and gives protection strategies in the form of affirmations, breathing, visualization, meditation, and even specific food recommendations that are grounding. I noticed that I was doing many of these things on my own, but her list was more extensive and specific in terms of how to protect myself from being over stimulated.

Being sober from alcohol when I was in social and over stimulating situations, I developed new patterns. I would go outside. I would turn to my pouch of essential oils, stress remedies and crystals. After reading Judith's book, I also had a "grounding and earthing visualization," a "shielding visualization for empaths," and the "opening to a higher power protective strategy." These would help me feel further grounded, alleviate the feelings of overstimulation, protect me from picking up negative energy from others, and connect me to myself and to God.

If you think you may be an empath, I highly recommend this book. It has been a true survival guide for me. Like many things, these techniques take practice, faith, and inner strength. Similar to other good practices that work over time—a healthy diet, exercise, and meditation—they take time to incorporate into your lifestyle. They aren't foolproof, but they are powerful and effective.

Every journey to healing and overcoming addiction is unique. There are certainly people who would not consider themselves empaths who struggle with addiction. Addicts turn to their various addictions for different reasons, and there are multiple ways to remedy these addictions. Addiction, disease and dysfunction are rampant in our modern fast paced society. It is easy to see how society can lead to these. However, the darkness of these destructive paths can reveal a process of discovery, and overcoming them can be a gift and an opportunity to see the light. Ultimately, I pray that those struggling with addiction realize the deep underlying message of what their addiction is telling them. I am so grateful I got to the bottom of mine.

For so many years, people were used to seeing a drink in my hand. Therefore, declining a cocktail and telling people I no longer drink was— and still is at times—a bit awkward. Although it has gotten much easier, it can be tricky to be in social situations where alcohol is being consumed. I try to be simple with my response and selective in bringing up the fact I don't drink anymore. Often, people become defensive and feel the need to justify their own drinking habits. I try to quickly tell them their relationship with alcohol is none of my business. I once enjoyed drinking, so I understand the appeal. I then internally surrender my judgment. How others choose to navigate their behaviors is for them to discover. After years and years, I am glad I found my way, and I wish others well on their journey.

Abstaining was the easiest way for me to handle my relationship with alcohol, but food was a bit trickier because you can't abstain from it. Even though I lost weight and have been maintaining it for the past several years, it is still something I deal with every day. It is always harder to manage in overstimulating social situations. As I get caught up in the party, I lose the connection to myself. I feel the urge to mindlessly graze on foods I would rarely eat otherwise. Every time I get the urge to eat or go somewhere where food is available—restaurants and people's homes—I have been getting better at recognizing this pattern, and I notice how I turn to food to help ground me or calm the anxious nerves that I no longer remedy with alcohol.

With everything that goes on at a party, it can be hard to stop and take the time to check in with myself and ask how I am feeling: good, bad, overwhelmed, anxious, or even bored? I pause and reconnect to why I am there—whether it is to connect with friends or family or because the kids want to be there. This pause and reconnection empowers me and allows me to then feel grounded and resilient. I look at the foods I want to eat and try not to restrict myself. I also consider what will best serve my body and mind. I have seen over and over how sugar and processed foods seem to make me feel even more disconnected and send my thoughts astray. Coffee has been a good companion at parties. If my energy feels low, it gives me a boost. I continue to work on this, and when it feels too overwhelming or I make poor food choices, I turn to God and ask for ease and comfort in my skin. This usually also allows me to feel self-compassion and forgiveness, and to know that I am doing the best I can.

I'm grateful that I have come to the understanding that the only way to truly fill the void is with self-love. Self-love can be hard to feel sometimes, especially when my energy is low. Fatigue and low energy will quickly gain momentum and lead to feelings of insecurity and inadequacy. It can morph into negative mind chatter resulting in feelings of shame. It's amazing what my ego manages to whisper in my ear before I am able to realize that the downward spiral of negative emotions is just my ego's attempts to tear me down.

Often I notice the pattern of seeking the approval and love of others, and then I turn in and realize the only love that matters is my own. I make the decision to love and forgive myself for petty thoughts and feelings. I think back to *A Course in Miracles* and realize that God loves me regardless of what I do and say. God has mercy on me and my dysfunctional patterns. He isn't judging me. I can release the judgments of others and of myself. I am the source of love—the booze and the food are not. So many of us struggle in the void, and my prayer is that everyone may find a path to better, more positive, outcomes.

My abstinence from alcohol is a wonderful reminder of the miracle of the transplant and my subsequent transformative breakthrough. I am thankful I had such an obvious pause, excuse, and opportunity to stop drinking. Without it, I'm not sure I would have done it. I probably would have been okay, since alcohol wasn't destroying my life, but the clarity, connectedness, and evolution I have experienced as a result are epic!

My connection to my true self has become deeper and more authentic now that I am no longer cloudy from booze. I am better able to follow my intuition which leads me to a deeper discovery of myself and the world around me. I am free to experience, more fully, all of the exciting adventures I have always been drawn to.

At an AA meeting I attended, someone said, "An alcoholic is a person whose life gets better after they stop drinking." The label of *alcoholic* and whether it applies is irrelevant. I can honestly say my life has gotten way better since I stopped drinking. That says a lot, because I had some pretty damn good times partying. I stopped going to AA meetings. They had served me well. I was feeling strong and resilient. It was now time to do the work on my own, and in my own way. I developed my own unique toolbox that has helped me greatly. I love knowing that if I ever need the support of AA meetings, they are waiting for me right down the block—and even at the beach.

# CHAPTER 9

# Spiritual Perseverance

By the fall of 2018, we were getting back into a groove: the kids at school, Ken back at work, and me sixty days without a drink. I was fully healed and reintegrating into society. I was ready to get back to my writing and to contemplating what meaningful work might mean for me going forward.

During our time in New York I had continued my daily morning pages and dabbled in some projects here and there, but the work on my book had come to a temporary pause. Now that I was healing on so many levels and feeling reinvigorated, it was time to get back to the therapeutic work that had prepared me for my transformation and had held my hand through it.

After so much had changed, getting reacquainted took some time. I went back to my *Artist's Way* affirmations: "I am a channel for God's creativity, and my work comes to good," "As I create and listen, I will be led," and "Great Creator, I will take care of the quantity, You take care of the quality." These affirmations helped with the pressure and fear of creating. When I started reading the book, almost a year prior, the author often referred to her recovery in AA. A lot of the language of addiction recovery and creative recovery overlapped. From my new perspective, I could now more fully appreciate the connection the author, Julia Cameron, was making, because I too was experiencing a new relationship with sobriety, creativity, and God. I felt as though they were interwoven.

I noticed when I successfully aligned myself with God, the writing would come flowing out. When I was in a more resistant state of fatigue, fear and insecurity, the old voices of "Who are you to write a book?" would return and cramp me up. The affirmations helped me stay aligned.

My faith was strong, especially when I recalled the synchronicity that had gotten me this far: discovering *The Artist's Way*, my subsequent process of creative recovery, the kidney transplant, sobriety from alcohol, and all the transformations along the way. It all felt so miraculous. My connection to the purity of my vision reassured me that forces higher than myself were indeed connected to all of the creativity flowing through me.

I was raised as a Christian and have a deep reverence for Jesus, who preached forgiveness and love. Christianity was the foundation on which my spiritual nature was built, but I didn't feel moved to practice it any longer. Even so, after many years of not attending church, I still wanted the bigger life milestones—our wedding and the birth of our children—to be spiritual in nature. We wrote our own wedding ceremony, and a dear friend with a Christian background performed it. A few months after Eliza's birth, we had a birth celebration at a Unitarian church in the town I grew up in. Madeleine had a similar type of celebration; a Unitarian pastor from the same church performed a brief ceremony at a restaurant. It was liberating to honor these events in a spiritual way but on our own terms.

Feeling more connected than ever to my spiritual path, I resumed working on my book. As I started writing, I fell into a rhythm that seemed to come naturally to me. I would wake up early, write my morning pages, and meditate. This would set the stage for the day ahead. Giving myself this personal time allowed me to connect more easily with my children and address their needs, feed them breakfast, make their lunches and help them get ready for school.

After driving the kids to school, I would release myself from the duties of motherhood and return home to work on my book. I would write for a few hours and then take a walk to clear my head. Being in nature, seeing the trees, listening to the birds and especially being near the water would restore me. Then it was time to pick up the kids and address after school activities, dinner, bath and bed.

The rhythm of my daily routine felt light and easy, and coupled with the writing I was doing and my meditation practices, it all combined to create a very satisfying synchronicity. I felt gratitude for this newfound ease and contentment. I discovered that my excess mind chatter could be placed in my morning pages or released during my walks. In this way, it became easier to sort petty egoic thoughts from the truth of what I really wanted to express. I had found an outlet, a way of working and of being that allowed me to feel I was being heard. My introverted nature had been preventing me from expressing myself. Now, working on my book, I felt like my thoughts had a home. This gave me a monumental sense of freedom.

The connection between spirituality and creativity continued to reveal itself to me. A few months before the surgery, during an energy clearing session conducted by my cousin, she asked her pendulum if my creative flow was blocked. I knew before I heard the answer that it was not. I believe creativity is innate in all of us; it's our process of translation that can get stuck. The creative flow comes from God, or if you prefer, Source Energy, and our task is to be open to it, to be receptive.

I felt certain the Divine energy that I was channeling into this book was pure and without ego; it didn't require acceptance or seek publication. However, it did yearn for expansion and was flowing through me seeking an outlet. I felt an insistent urge to write. I don't think it's an exaggeration to say my writing came to feel like my souls destiny. Knowing this helped me work past my resistance and my fear of failure. I intuitively knew the source of my work protected it from ever truly failing. My ego wanted my project to be successful, but my soul, which is an extension of God, knew deep down it already was a success, because this book is now sitting in your hands, not sitting in my computer because I gave up or was too fearful to finish.

I am so grateful for my transformational experiences. They culminated in the transplant and landed me on this spiritual path. My previous path used to look to the external for pleasure. A year before the transplant, I would drop off the kids with their grandparents and run to go out and get a drink or seek some other external stimuli to feel good. I wanted to celebrate the feeling of freedom, and celebration meant alcohol.

After the transplant, I still made that same drop off, and I still felt the need to celebrate, but the adventures that satisfied my soul had changed. From that fall to this day, it has excited me to go home and get back to my writing or to continue my spiritual path work in some other way. Whether taking a walk on the beach, going out with Ken and exploring something new, or an outing that revolves around the arts, while the environment may have shifted from bars and alcohol, the satisfaction and contentment with how I use my personal time has increased tenfold.

As October continued, I was on a mission. I was a writer working diligently on a book. Although it was premature, I wondered how I would eventually publish the book. I had the option to self publish or to pursue the path of traditional publishing, but I knew practically nothing about either option. That's when I discovered Balboa Press. I had always been inspired by Louise Hay and many other authors that published books under Hay House, a publishing company Louise Hay had founded. I was delighted when I found out Hay House had a division, Balboa Press, that sells self-publishing packages.

I had been working on the book for almost a year. The many hours I put in were deeply satisfying for my soul, yet they weren't generating income in a traditional sense. How then to pay for the publishing package? I didn't panic; instead, I recalled the abundance and prosperity training work I had done a few years back. I was beginning to identify myself as a writer, but I still possessed a skill set that could generate income: physical therapy! The universe, once again, had my back. I could do freelance work as a physical therapist to raise the money.

The decision to self publish gave me the inspiration and confidence to start practicing physical therapy again, this time on my own terms. Prior to my children being born, I had worked many years in hospitals, rehab centers, outpatient clinics, and home care agencies. I enjoyed the work, but something was always missing. I would change jobs and those same feelings would return. When I became a mother, I had to put my work on pause, not because I was forced to but because my children needed me, and because I fervently believe that being a mother is meaningful work. I returned to work part time when Eliza was nine months old and worked until I gave birth to Maddy.

Caring for two young children and relocating from New York City to Hampton Bays was a full-time job. It was fulfilling in and of itself. However, as my children aged and needed me a fraction less than when they were infants, I started picking up per diem physical therapy work at a local outpatient clinic. The work was great, conveniently located, flexible, and paid me well. Working at the clinic felt familiar, and helping my patients improve their functional status and quality-of-life was certainly meaningful, and was why I went into the field in the first place. However, there was a downside. Going back to work reminded me of the feelings I had had years ago. Regardless of where I worked, it was hard to keep my vibration up or stay grounded. External forces beyond my control such as documentation, insurance regulations, and over scheduling would leave me feeling over stimulated and overwhelmed. I assumed these feelings came with the territory. Doing the job I was trained to do came with time-consuming distractions that left me unable to fully serve my patients. Being back at work after being a mom only magnified these frustrations. Caring for my children and managing a home is a very focused and satisfying endeavor. I had no trouble giving it my full attention, but as the children got older, I felt the need to put my training back to use.

Achieving a deeper understanding of myself and learning that I was an empath and what that meant, helped me to understand that, for someone like me, working in a distracting environment was over stimulating—and not in a good way. Not being able to focus all of my attention on my patients frustrated me and this lead, once again, to that all too familiar empty void I had so often felt. From my new transformative vantage point, and with the opportunity to change the way I worked, I paused and tuned into my inner voice. Guided by Spirit, I sought to practice physical therapy in a way that was more conducive to my patients and to myself. As I reflected on this, I used my writing as a therapeutic tool and allowed the answers to unfold. Stepping back into the flow allowed those answers to come with ease.

One day, I attended my first yoga class since the surgery. I had been walking and doing yoga stretches on my own but was ready to try a studio class. Initially I was timid, but to my pleasant surprise, the owner, who I knew but hadn't connected with since prior to the surgery, embraced me with open arms and was eager to share my story of donating my kidney with the class. Her support was encouraging, and it evolved into her recruiting me to teach anatomy for her yoga teacher training program and would allow me to utilize a treatment room in her studio designated for various practitioners. This made it possible for me to offer private sessions to clients. It was a glorious opportunity to make the transition I always felt was my calling, shifting from traditional physical therapy to holistic physical therapy.

Shortly before I began working on my Doctorate in Physical Therapy, I had gotten a tattoo of the Chinese symbol meaning 'healer' on the inside of my left ankle. Entering the occupation of physical therapy, I felt a deeper calling to heal, and now I could do just that. With this new opportunity I could work one on one with clients in a quiet and calm environment. This allowed me to stay grounded and facilitate a connection to my intuition and to Spirit. Working privately with clients, we more efficiently got to the root of the problem. With this new freedom and ease, as well as my deeper spiritual connection, I could feel the healing coming through, healing my clients as well as myself. Before, I would feel drained after working with patients, feeling like I gave them all my energy. Now I realized there was no scarcity. The healing energy from Source was unlimited. On top of it all, this created income, which helped publish my book!

This was a paradigm shift from the more rigid, academic, and textbook way of practicing physical therapy. My journey to inner discovery had started as an educational path led by my head. I was fortunate to have access to quality public education and higher education. I looked to my high school teachers and college professors for guidance. With each graduation I felt wiser. However, the well-known phrase by Laozi, "The more you know, the less you understand," was definitely true for me.

As a college student, the pressure to retain knowledge resulted in a reliance on mental strength, hard work and stamina, but this reliance took a toll on my connection to a higher power. The pressure was intense. I relied purely on myself. When I didn't measure up I felt shame. I was isolated. My Bachelor of Science and Doctorate in Physical Therapy degrees encouraged evidence-based medicine and made it hard to believe in miracles. I watched the way institutions I worked in operated in a secular manner. As part of my required continuing education, I traveled to national conferences, where I attended lectures given by top medical professionals. The science they taught was exact, but the moments I remember most are those when the lecturer came to the unknown questions and paused. So it was a relief when I found myself working at Columbia-Presbyterian, one of the top hospitals in the country. I found it exciting that in addition to offering state of the art care and cutting edge procedures, they also incorporated holistic therapies and hosted support groups. I also found it comforting that they had a chapel. A dormant spark ignited every time I discovered and rediscovered the small window left for the consideration of what happens beyond the physical.

Whereas I lit up and felt excited about these more esoteric influences, there were others who thought this way of thinking strange. The students I sat alongside in my collegiate classrooms, and later my professional colleagues, and others I met along the way, all seemed so sure of themselves. I felt the people around me saw black and white, whereas I saw shades of gray. In the song "Shades of Gray," Billy Joel sings, "The only people I fear are those who never have doubts." I was often overwhelmed with doubt and questioning the certainty that others took for granted.

As my head filled with expensive higher education, I felt more unsure and disconnected from my intuition. I would read randomized control trials, a type of scientific study, and it seemed to me the researchers too often remained uncertain about the questions they had set out to answer. The only certainty was that further research was needed. And then news headlines and people around me would reference these scientific studies, which only resulted in more shades of gray. At the time I felt frustrated by all of this, but now my connection to Spirit has helped ground and stabilize me.

The transplant and my transformational journey helped me shift from my head to a more holistic way of working, using science in a more creative and inclusive way. I remember my professors mentioning the phrase "the art of physical therapy." I now realize it was years of experience in the field that allowed them to shift from novice to confident and experienced practitioners. Now, after so many years, I too had made this shift and found the freedom that came with it. I gave myself permission to lean on my intuition as an enhancement to the fact-based knowledge I had learned in school. The results were amazing! Combining my traditional physical therapy knowledge and experience with my newfound spiritual power allowed me to facilitate deeper and more productive healing.

Being a mom, running a household, writing my book, seeing private patients, and occasionally picking up per diem shifts at the clinic, I felt happier and more productive than I ever had at my nine-to-five jobs. I felt blessed to have the work versus the earlier years when I often dreaded going to work. Although my schedule was full, it came with a sense of freedom. If one of the children was unexpectedly ill or there was a school break, I was flexible and flowing to accommodate it. Most, if not all, mothers I know are world-class jugglers. At times I would feel overwhelmed by the number of balls I juggled, but because I was now my own boss I felt more in control and less victim to it.

The Thanksgiving after the transplant found our family more than ever filled with gratitude. We had so much to be thankful for. On Giving Tuesday, the Tuesday after Thanksgiving, the students at my daughters' school made a charming and heartwarming thermometer with the goal of raising money for the school. Giving Tuesday comes at the beginning of the holiday season and encourages charitable giving to not-for-profit organizations. As they met their goal, there was a lot of excitement in the air as the homemade thermometer with children's handwriting on it was colored in red all the way up to the top.

This inspired me. The next day, while the kids were at school, I made my own thermometer. I recycled an old piece of poster board I found in the basement and drew a large thermometer on it. At the top I put the dollar amount for the self-publishing package and included an extra 10 percent as a contribution to Donate Life. Years back, at the Abundance and Prosperity workshop, we discussed how in order to get we must give. Donate Life was an organization near and dear to my heart. I put the poster in my writing room behind the desk where I spent my days working on my book. I started taping photocopies of the paychecks I received from seeing private clients and teaching anatomy at the yoga studio, as well as checks I received from the per diem PT shifts at the clinic, onto the poster board.

While working on my thermometer, I heard the phone ringing in the other room. When I picked it up, it was another prospective private client who had seen one of my PT brochures at the yoga studio. We spoke and scheduled a session. It was thrilling to see that my project was working! It gave me faith that I could finance my vision project with work that was meaningful and aligned with what I was writing about in my book.

My belief in a higher power provided me with the inspiration that kept me going. Still, resistance would regularly pop up. It was the French philosopher Pierre Teilhard de Chardin who said, 'We are not human beings having a spiritual experience. We are spiritual beings having a human experience." I felt this was true, and part of the human experience is frequent encounters with resistance.

Resistance is the biggest obstacle to spiritual perseverance—and to pretty much any other creative endeavor. Coming across the book, *The War of Art*, by Steven Pressfield, helped me navigate resistance. The author explains how resistance comes in many common forms, including procrastination, unhappiness, victimhood and fundamentalism, just to name a few. He also states in his book that resistance is universal, it feeds on fear, but it can be beaten. "Real writers know that it's not the writing part that is hard; it is the sitting down part". This comforted me as I started noticing a trend: resist, create, peace, resist, create, peace, and so on. The passage titled 'What a Writer's Day Feels Like' felt extremely familiar: "waking with a gnawing sensation of dissatisfaction and resistance in their gut". I too would wake up in the morning feeling a sense of duty to work on my book, only to confront a myriad of resistance to finding the time for editing, revising, trying to clearly state my thoughts, organizing sentences, substituting words, and wondering if it was all even worth it.

After his writing session was over for that day, Pressfield felt the proud joy of beating resistance: "for today at least because tomorrow, rest assured, resistance will be back." It would be easy to give up, but a writer should resist the urge to quit. If you feel you were born to write, Pressman asserts, you should do it. Being creative is not a selfish thing to do; rather it is a gift, a contribution to the greater good. Pressman's book helped me to better understand the urgency I felt to create and inspired in me the spiritual perseverance required to stay the course. For me, the word 'perseverance' had always conjured up an image of a sweaty, panting athlete struggling to win a big fight and defying all odds (and maybe an image of Sylvester Stallone in Rocky IV). I suppose that association goes back to the pressure and adrenaline of playing competitive volleyball and softball in high school as a Paramus Spartan.

One day, while working, it occurred to me to look up the difference between motivation and inspiration. When you compare the two definitions, motivation is the reason one has for acting and is an outside pulling force, whereas inspiration is the process of being mentally stimulated to do or feel something and is an inside driving force. I flashed back to being a teenager, running miles in practice, doing repetitive drills over and over, and the pain of stinging hands holding a metal bat when it made contact with a softball on a cold spring training morning. Our coaches would motivate us; if we wanted to win, this is what it took! My coaches meant well, and looking back there was value and plenty of fun times playing high school sports. However, it also occurs to me that I was being pushed by outside forces, learning lessons that I've had to unlearn.

Aligning myself with Spirit while writing this book gave me the confidence to allow internal inspiration to guide me rather than external motivation. This brought an ease to the process and to the work itself. Regardless of the many hours I put in, I wouldn't describe them as hard. This endeavor has not been the scene of a sweaty athlete pushing herself to lift the heavy barbell with a coach yelling in the background. It has been an inner calling which, to be sure, has definitely had its own challenging obstacles of resistance, ego and fear. To overcome those forces I had to always remind myself to surrender and to allow my creative energy to flow.

As I was writing my book—and living my life—I began to notice that I rarely used the word motivate anymore. However, the word inspiration summoned a grateful feeling that was occurring abundantly in all areas of my life. Inspiration and gratitude were themes in my book, and as I went on to other aspects of my day, I would see these themes play out all around me. My children inspired me to strive to be a good mom. My husband inspired me to strive to be a good wife. Inspirational figures in my community, locally and globally, inspired me to strive to be a good citizen. Authors I read and listened to inspired me to understand myself more deeply and to seek work that went beyond money in my pocket, to discover work that would nourish my soul. Through all this, I experienced another paradigm shift, away from the earlier days on the volleyball court trying to be the best and win, to now following the inspiration and seeing what manifested.

With my inner voice as my new coach, I was waking up with lots of energy. My morning pages served as a road map for the day. I would get the kids off to school and was eager to get to my writing room and get to work. Some days when my energy was low, my inner voice encouraged me to work past it, drag myself out of bed, push against the rainy morning and resist groggy feelings. At other times, when I was having a rough day, my inner voice would advise that I give in rather than push against or ignore what I was feeling. Inspirational speaker and author, Esther Hicks, whose work is focused on the Law of Attraction, suggests taking a nap when your vibration feels low or the momentum of a problem is too high and difficult to face. Initially this notion hit a nerve. Take a nap? What about the hard work? Isn't taking a nap giving up and giving in? Hicks, however, maintains that taking a nap is often a necessary pause, a resetting of the momentum.

Hard work is encouraged in our society as a precursor to success. I was taught to work hard by teachers, coaches and my very hardworking parents. In fact, when I thought of hard work, the image of my father came to mind. As a retired general contractor, he woke up early every day and worked hard, the same way his father did. On weekends, he and my Mom worked endlessly on home improvements and yard work, taking impeccable pride in the quality of our home. I have certainly put in many hours at numerous jobs throughout the years and that has brought valuable experience to my life. I also pushed out my two babies, and that, along with the sleepless nights of caring for them, is probably some of the hardest work I will ever experience. Giving birth felt like a calling I had come into this life to do. It taught me that work could be hard and meaningful at the same time.

These reflections on resistance, hard work and motivation, seen from my new spiritual vantage point, were all coming together in the writing of my book. My early morning meditations and morning writing set the pace and guided me. When I was moving too fast, juggling too much, working too hard and obsessing over my to-do list, I prayed and advised myself to "let go and let God." I did the seemingly endless human work of researching, preparing and planning, and then I did the even harder work of going with the flow of God's will, which wasn't hard when I truly let go. The process of surrender helped me handle the pressure and perfection of what I could realistically accomplish day-to-day and kept me going as the days continued. I accepted that I was only capable of so much. I soothed myself when I lost my way.

In order to tune back into my inner voice, I learned to take frequent breaks throughout the day, even if only through a few deep breaths. Regardless of my pace, going too fast or willing myself to slow down, by the evening I was exhausted. When my fatigue was high, so too was my resistance, and the negative mind chatter in my head would sound like a board meeting with lots of angry shouting voices. Those were the times in the past when I used to turn to alcohol or food to seek comfort. Sometimes the old athlete in me would resurface, and I could hear my old coaches trying to motivate me: "If you want to write a book, you better do more work!" At such times my inner voice would respond: 'Surrender. Surrender to the evening demons. Surrender, and go to bed. Let go. Sleep.' In the morning, refreshed, I could feel the light once again, and inspired, I returned to my writing.

By the end of December and into the New Year of 2019, my spiritual perseverance paid off. My book was coming along. The paychecks taped on my thermometer were growing. And amazingly, I got the opportunity to celebrate my spiritual perseverance with an incredible invitation to go to Sri Lanka on a Buddhist Meditation Retreat!!!

# CHAPTER 10

# Sri Lanka

On January 18th, 2019, we landed at the Bandaranaike International Airport in Sri Lanka's capital city, Colombo. I was extremely fatigued after traveling for more than thirty hours; however, I also felt exhilarated arriving at such an exotic destination. As I deplaned, I felt a warm breeze on my face and admired the lush landscape of the pear-shaped island country. We entered a bus and were transported to the terminal. I was eager to see the terminal building and compare it to the impressively modern one I was in five hours earlier in Doha, Qatar.

If you had asked me a year ago where Sri Lanka was located, I wouldn't have been able to tell you. After preparing for the trip and doing some research, I learned that the country rests in the Indian Ocean a few degrees above the equator. It is roughly the size of West Virginia, and India is its closest neighbor.

As our group—most of whom I was still becoming acquainted with— walked into the terminal, I didn't see any shops or newsstands. I saw only what I can describe as a sea of paparazzi and flashing lights coming from a line of photographers on both sides of the hallway. They were documenting our entrance into the country. We were accompanying Bhante Nanda, a Buddhist monk. He was the reason we were here. Still, we were very surprised by all this attention. Beautiful orchid necklaces were delicately placed over our necks. I ask myself, *is this a dream?* There was a lot of commotion and more flashing lights. The pleasant surprises continued as we were ushered into the airport's luxurious VIP lounge. It felt like we were traveling with a Hollywood movie star, except the movie star was a monk. Over the next ten days, I learned why he was being welcomed this way.

As fate and good fortune would have it, I sat next to Bhante Nanda on the second flight from Doha to Colombo. This flight was a mere five hours compared to the more than twelve-hour flight from New York to Doha. I boarded the plane and entered the row of my assigned seat. Then, looking at the oncoming passengers, I watched as Bhante Nanda walked down the aisle in his bright red robes and sat in the seat next to me. I was excited and nervous to have a monk sitting beside me.

"Good morning," he said with a warm smile.

"Good morning" I replied. I had met Bhante Nanda at our informational trip meetings at the Long Island Buddhist Meditation Center (LIBMC). I also attended meditation classes he led at the center's temple, located in Aquebogue, eleven miles from my home in Hampton Bays. A few years ago, a friend of mine, Don Jayamaha, had asked me to meet him at Grange Hall. Grange Hall served as a church until 1860, and then it was converted to a school. Over the years, Grange Hall has been used as a gathering place for local farmers, a center for dances and social gatherings, and as a homeless shelter. The historic landmark is now the LIBMC. Don had arranged the purchase of the deteriorated building with the intention of renovating it. When Don told me of his plan to convert the disheveled space into a Buddhist temple, I was a bit skeptical. I was not aware at the time that the vision was fueled by his partnership with Bhante Nanda.

Bhante Nanda came to New York City in 2001 from Sri Lanka by invitation from the chief priest of the New York Buddhist Temple. Well educated, and a monk since age eleven, Bhante Nanda came to realize one of the most effective things he could offer Americans, particularly New Yorkers, was the ability to relax and enjoy life through meditation.

By 2008, Bhante Nanda had established a thriving sangha, or community, at a house in Port Jefferson, which had kindly been donated by Don and his wife, Dr. Sharmini Jayamaha. As the community grew and thrived, they needed a bigger space. Classes were being held temporarily at Don's wife's medical office. I saw a flyer and attended a class, whereupon I discovered that Dr. Sharmini Jayamaha was a colleague of my husband's. As I became better acquainted with The Jaymahas, I began to realize how dedicated they both were. They were fully committed to hosting the meditation classes and to creating a Buddhist community on the East End of Long Island.

Sitting on the plane, I was a bit shy and unfamiliar with how to respectfully and properly interact with a monk. I didn't know Bhante Nanda very well yet. I had so many questions. However, since I had the deepest reverence for such a peaceful individual, I refrained. I did not want my uninformed questions to come off as disrespectful. Instead, I took the Sri Lanka guidebook I had borrowed from the library out of my bag, intending to do more research on the foreign land I was about to enter. Bhante Nanda pointed to the picture on the cover of the book and explained to me it was a picture of oil lamps, the kind that are commonly seen in Sri Lanka's many Buddhist temples. And so began a pleasant conversation with Bhante Nanda about Sri Lanka. When the flight attendant handed us breakfast trays, I told Bhante it was the first time I'd had breakfast with a monk. He smiled, and I felt the most peaceful presence radiating from him.

That was the first of many opportunities I had over the ten-day trip to interact with the Sri Lankan monk and see first hand how truly remarkable he was. It was no wonder the photographers and reporters had lined up to document his return to his homeland. Bhante Nanda had dedicated his life to the dharma teachings and to serving his country. The establishment of LIBMC was evidence that he had indeed gone beyond the motherland to offer these teachings to the world, and our group's arrival was evidence that his work was being received.

When I signed up for the trip, I thought it would be nice to travel and see Sri Lanka and the Buddhist temples. From our grand entrance, it was clear we were part of something much bigger. Bhante Nanda's humility would never indicate any of this. He calmly smiled when photographers snapped photos. He answered the reporters' questions succinctly and warmly. With stillness and grace, he stood quietly while people from all over the country bowed at his feet.

The rest of our time at the Colombo airport was spent in the carpeted and comfortable VIP lounge where we were served tea and had access to private bathrooms. It was a perfect place to freshen up. Our fabulous welcome was topped off further when we handed our passports to personnel who then retrieved our bags from customs. I had flown to foreign countries many times and often waited in long lines at customs and baggage claim. This experience was the opposite. I had never experienced such an easeful entrance into a foreign country. Our luggage was then loaded onto a deluxe air-conditioned travel bus on which we would spend the next ten days traveling through Sri Lanka. I smiled when I saw the bus. I knew it would be the perfect 'office' for all the writing and working on my book I intended to do. This wonderful entrance set the tone for the magic we were about to experience every day on this extraordinary adventure.

Prior to the trip, I had heard about a planned event with the president of Sri Lanka, but with all the preparation for the trip and the extensive itinerary, the information didn't fully register. As we pulled out of the airport, I became aware of an official white Mercedes government vehicle and two police motorcycles driving in front of our bus. Since we were guests of the president, the motorcade had been assigned to guide us through rush hour traffic in order to expedite our trip to the hotel. I had been in Sri Lanka for less than two hours and felt more like royalty than I ever had. After our grand entrance and escort, I was overflowing with gratitude being a part of this experience.

The next day—after some much needed rest—we were up early and met in the lobby. As we went out to board the bus, the incredibly friendly driver bowed his head, held his hands in a prayer position and said, *"Ayubowan."* Ayubowan means "long life" or "may you live long" in Sinhalese, the official language of Sri Lanka. It was such an incredible way to start the day. We were all delighted when we realized that every time we got on or off the bus, which could be half a dozen times or more a day, this greeting was to be a part of a regular occurrence. First, there would be a greeting from the driver's assistant standing at the base of the steps to the bus; then there would be a second greeting from the driver as he sat at the large steering wheel; next we would be blessed with a warm smile from Bhante Nanda, as well as from a monk from Bangladesh who was traveling with us; and as I made my way down the aisle, the receiving line of warm heartfelt welcomes continued as I met the gaze of my fellow traveling companions, who had come from as far away as Singapore. I never tired of this wonderful recurring ritual, which was the beginning of many joyful rituals we would encounter on the trip.

On our first days adventure, we headed two hours south to the tip of

Sri Lanka, to the forest monastery where Bhante Nanda had studied. I enjoyed the breathtaking landscape: the paddy fields, the lakes with white and pink lotus flowers, and the water lilies—Sri Lanka's national flower. We took pictures and enjoyed listening to our knowledgeable tour guide in the front of the bus. He spoke into a microphone teaching us about the culture of Sri Lanka, identifying the flora and fauna we were seeing, and answered our endless questions. As we rode along, the views inspired me, and I wrote in my leather bound journal, the one my sister in law had given me for Christmas. I didn't know at the time of receiving this lovely gift that I would even be going to Sri Lanka. And here I was, less than a month later, writing in my journal and gazing out the window. Life was glorious!

We arrived at the Wathurawila Meditation Center, a forest monastery north of the city of Galle where Bhante Nada had begun his training as a monk. The nearby villagers had come to welcome Bhante Nanda and his array of international guests. We were given lotus flowers and betel leaves as we exited the bus, which we were to present as offerings to the Buddha. As requested, we were dressed in white for the occasion. We lined up two by two to walk down the jungle path and up the stairs to the temple. We saw monkeys and remained quiet as we walked past the rows of striped flags of blue, yellow, red, white and orange. We entered the space, continued all the way to the shrine, presented our flowers and bowed. We were reverent and could feel how sacred this beautiful place was. The villagers and the center were honored to have Bhante visit. In turn, Bhante was honored to have the center where he had started his spiritual life as a young monk welcome him in this way. And those of us traveling with Bhante felt blessed to be included in such a meaningful occasion.

We left the shrine and went through an adjacent doorway that opened into a large space where a ceremony honoring Bhante Nanda was to be conducted. I immediately noticed another statue of the Buddha. This statue was much larger than the one in the shrine. It rested on a platform at the front of the temple, reaching almost as high as the ceiling. It even had flashing lights going around it. We sat in chairs that were neatly arranged in rows on one side of the room. As I sat down, I saw rows of young boys in their monks' robes seated across from us on the other side of the room. I also noticed an oil lamp like the one Bhante had pointed out on the cover of my guidebook.

As the ceremony began, I directed my attention to the center of the room where distinguished guests were seated. Among them were Bhante Nanda, his more senior monk teachers, and Don. We listened, mesmerized, as the monks and groups of villagers seated in the back of the room chanted the opening Buddhist invocations in Pali, the classic language of Buddhism. It was melodic to listen to and set the tone for the ceremony. Next came a speech welcoming us, which was delivered in Sinhalese then translated into English. The microphone was passed down the line to the more senior monk teachers who acknowledged the work of Bhante Nanda. Again the speeches were translated into English, after which an award was presented to Bhante Nanda. I was delighted when an award was also presented to Don Jayamaha, my friend who had invited me on this trip. It's worth noting here that prior to the trip, Bhante Nanda had requested that, if he was going to be honored, Don should be honored as well, because there would be no LIBMC without Don. At the end of the ceremony, donated gifts which we had brought with us from America were presented to all the monks at the temple. The younger monks received gift bags with pencils, notebooks and chocolates. The older monks were presented with newly wrapped robes.

When we were packing our bags for the trip, we were asked to only pack one of our two allowed checked bags with personal items so that our second checked bag could be used for carrying the donated gifts we intended to distribute at the various events we would be attending. We were happy to comply. Throughout the trip, it was very gratifying—and certainly appropriate—to be able to offer these gifts as a token of our appreciation for the generous hospitality we received.

After the ceremony, we walked around in a more casual fashion and explored the beautiful meditation center. The small, simple buildings were spread out in the open natural setting. We walked up stone steps to a giant Buddha statue, which had been carved out of the side of the mountain, and bowed to it. We took pictures to capture the magical moment and were careful not to have our backs facing the statue, which was a sign of disrespect. We enjoyed breathtaking views of the center, the stupa (shrine), and the forest. After the hot and steep climb, we were offered refreshing coconut water straight out of King coconuts. It was the most incredible way to spend our first full day in Sri Lanka.

I wasn't sure that first day could be topped. I was wrong. On the second day, we stayed in the city of Colombo and attended a special event at the Bandaranaike Memorial International Conference Hall. Our bus drove past the security gates to the beautiful state-of-the-art convention center that looked as though the United Nations could meet there. Security was everywhere. We got off the bus and proceeded past metal detectors. We had received word that the president of Sri Lanka would be in attendance. The multitude of people excitedly streaming past us indicated that he had indeed arrived. We entered a large and very impressive conference room. We watched as the room filled to overflowing. There were photographers and media reporters documenting and covering everything.

The ceremony opened with the singing of the national anthem of Sri Lanka and, to our surprise, the National Anthem of the United States. The ceremony was to honor the work of Bhante Nanda and the establishment of the LIBMC. We listened to heartfelt speeches in Sinhalese that were then translated into English. A member of our group stood up at the podium in front of the hundreds in attendance and eloquently spoke about her experiences at LIBMC. Then it was Bhante Nanda's turn. He stood with strength and grace and delivered a speech about his experience and journey as a monk. I got chills as he spoke of how we all share an inner desire for peace, contentment and happiness, and said this is what had fueled him to go beyond his motherland to a foreign land. Listening to his speech, and experiencing Bhante's humility and authenticity, made it obvious to me how he had achieved such great success in his endeavors and become the founder, Chief Abbot and President of LIBMC.

Bhante's dream had been to pursue a life of dharma service but not necessarily to come to America. When his teachers presented him with the opportunity to go to the United States, it was their mentorship and guidance which gave Bhante the support and encouragement he needed to do the work for which he was being honored at this incredible event. The power of the Buddha's teachings gave Bhante the inner strength required to lead a life of service and, as a result, a beautiful path unfolded before him. Once again, the gifts we had brought with us were dispersed to the more than eighty monks in attendance. We were all surprised when, in return, we received gifts as well: plaques to commemorate the special day. We were truly having a once-in-a-lifetime experience!

The next morning, on our third day, as I was on my way to breakfast, I looked down and saw a newspaper on the floor outside my hotel room. I smiled when I saw the picture on the front page of the president kneeling on a white cloth before Bhante and handing him an award. I cut out the photo, and when I got home hung it in my writing room.

On the fourth day, we left the urban streets of Colombo and headed three and a half hours inland to the heart of the island country. The hills gave way to mountains as we drove towards Kandy, the second largest city in Sri Lanka. It is referred to as the 'cultural capital'. We visited a museum and learned about the gem mining industry in Sri Lanka. Then we checked into our hotel. As we explored the grounds with our welcome drinks of papaya juice in hand, we noticed monkeys in the trees above the pool. That evening, we visited the most sacred temple in Sri Lanka: the Temple of the Tooth.

We had been in our white clothes multiple times by then and knew temple etiquette: removing our shoes, offering flowers and gifts, and bowing at the altar. The Temple of the Tooth was different. Sri Lankans and foreigners come here by the thousands. As we crossed over the moat leading to the temple, humanity swirled all around us. They had come to be in the presence of the sacred tooth relic of the Buddha. It was a crowded and chaotic scene. I observed mothers holding small babies. They had brought them here in order for the babies to receive the blessings of this sacred space. We stood in our white sarongs, which one of the local monks, Bhanti Samitha, had purchased and dressed us in prior to entering the temple. Most of us were already wearing white clothes, however, Bhante Samitha draped the white sarongs over our clothes to make sure that our whites were in perfect order. We were going to be let past the crowds and velvet ropes to visit the hidden shrine where the relic is located. This was a very special honor. The majority of visitors who come to the Temple of the Tooth do not get to see the relic and are merely content to be in its presence.

Before we could get to the relic, there was a lot of standing around and waiting in line. We did not mind; we were grateful to be getting this VIP experience. We slowly made our way up and down aisles, past many guards and waiting rooms until we finally reached the relic. You do not see the tooth; it is protected by bulletproof glass and housed in a gold casket, which contains a series of six other caskets of diminishing size. It was an extraordinary privilege and beyond thrilling to be in this sacred room with the holy relic.

Afterward, we had a puja (a religious ceremony) in a less crowded part of the temple. It was perfect to sit quietly and meditate in the energy of such a special temple. It was getting late by the time we left. We were exhausted; however, the evening was not over. The organizers of the trip, in coordination with the monks, were in the process of arranging for us to meet the head monk of the temple. I am certainly no expert in the Sri Lankan monk hierarchy, but I was told the monk we were about to meet was the Buddhist equivalent of the Pope. We got on the bus, rode a short way, walked down a dark alley and were ushered into a fairly modest establishment where the monk resided.

As I was getting more acquainted with the monks who were accompanying us, I had come to feel more comfortable being in their presence. However, meeting the head monk of the Temple of the Tooth felt different, and I was nervous. When it was my turn to approach him, I smiled, put my hands together in prayer and bowed as I had done many times on the trip. Only this time, my bow went further; I decided to bow to his feet.

A few days prior, while eating in a restaurant, I noticed the chef coming out of the kitchen and bowing to Bhante Nanda's feet—just as many others had done throughout the trip. What I came to love about the reverent behavior around monks was that there were guidelines but no hard and fast rules. I was never told to bow or how to act or what to believe. We were not required to be Buddhists in order to go on this trip. It was also not necessary to be a Buddhist to visit the many Buddhist temples or attend the ceremonies. In fact, if you had asked people on the trip what religion they were, you would have heard answers that included Catholic, Jewish, and those claiming they did not practice any religion.

At times I felt unsure I had earned all of this special treatment, but, eventually, I realized it didn't matter. Receiving all these privileges and experiencing the sacred moments of the trip, I freely chose to bow at the monk's feet out of respect and gratitude. Bhante Nanda would say that we all were deserving of the blessings. The lessons of the dharma teachings and benefits of meditation are available to all regardless of whether we claim to be Buddhist or not. This trip reaffirmed for me the notion of freedom that could exist in spiritual beliefs and practices. I was so happy I had done the work I had prior to the trip cultivating my own spiritual path.

After we had greeted the monk, gifts were offered and presented. The monk then spoke in Sinhalese with Bhante Nanda. We did not understand the conversation, but we could feel the warmth and see the friendly smiles. Toward the end of their conversation, the monk turned to us, and, through a translator, he asked us how we were enjoying Sri Lanka and what we thought of the Temple of the Tooth. We told him of the magnificence we experienced at the Temple and of our overall incredible stay in Sri Lanka. The honor in the room felt like a two-way street. Bhante Nanda and our group were clearly honored to be in the presence of this monk. It seemed equally true that the head monk was impressed to see one of his fellow monks go to America, establish a temple, then see him return accompanied by a group from all over the world and be honored by the President of Sri Lanka. This all paid tribute to the profound effects of the dharma teachings.

The next several days brought more magical excursions: a trip to a luscious spice garden, a visit to the Dambulla Cave temples, an elephant safari, a visit to ruins complete with monkeys, and many more pujas (spiritual ceremonies). One of our days started with a six o'clock meditation and puja under a sacred Sri Maha Bodhi Tree. The Buddha had attained enlightenment while sitting under a Bodhi Tree very much like this one. After the meditation, the local people thoughtfully—and impeccably—organized a beautiful white linen breakfast that was served on the riverbank. During another puja, we wrapped a 1,200-foot orange runner around one of the biggest shrines (stupas) in Sri Lanka.

There was also a moment of notable synchronicity that occurred during the trip. In Sri Lanka, many people make major life decisions based on readings by local astrologers. The first two nights of the trip, I had the honor of sharing a hotel room with a Sri Lankan native who had lived on Long Island for many years. She was an accomplished scientist by profession, but in her spare time she assisted Bhante Nanda at LIBMC. During an evening conversation, she was a bit timid in telling me she had arranged an appointment to get an astrology reading the next day during a small rare window of free time we had. I assured her that, after attending

146

various healing and energy clearing sessions and psychic readings myself, I was no stranger to metaphysical work, and I didn't think it was in the least bit odd. In fact, I asked if I could join her in getting a reading myself.

We took a tuk tuk (a three-wheeled motorized scooter) to the other side of the city. It was quite convenient that my Sri Lankan friend was able to speak Sinhalese and communicate with the driver. We had chosen the driver by chance on the street in front of the hotel, and it was unclear if he knew where we were going. My friend's cell phone battery had died, which felt like our only lifeline, since mine did not work in Sri Lanka. I had brave faith that we would get there safely, but, for a moment or two, I recalled the precarious times when I was in India almost ten years earlier.

We finally pulled up to the building where the astrologer worked. We were unsure if he would be there since our appointment times had not been firmly set. We walked past a small waiting room with a few Sri Lankans in it and into a small poorly lit office. The office had two chairs, a bookshelf and a desk. There were no crystal balls or anything out of the ordinary. The astrologer was a normal-looking, middle-aged Sri Lankan man wearing glasses. During the readings, he spent most of the time staring at his dated looking computer.

My Sri Lankan friend received her reading first. It was mostly in Sinhalese, and she filled me in occasionally. She brought sheets of paper from previous readings that she wanted updates and clarifications on. This wasn't some kooky whim. This was a purposeful visit; she was here to verify that her karma and her family's karma were in good standing. She seemed relieved and satisfied with what the astrologer had to say. After about thirty minutes, it was my turn.

Since the astrologer did not speak any English, and the entire reading was done in Sinhalese, I was grateful to my friend for her expert translation. The astrologer was very specific in asking questions about the exact place and time of my birth. As he entered that information into his computer, he printed out a natal chart, which showed the results of all my karma. The two pages showed many diagrams and coordinates and contained lots of Sinhalese writing. The astrologer spoke with my friend for a while, then they would pause and she would translate.

Early on in the reading, my friend translated the phrase "take care of my kidney". I asked if she had told him that I had donated my kidney, but she said no. When she translated back to the astrologer, explaining my husband's transplant, he smiled and seemed pleased with himself. The astrologer also told me that my moon was in a good place, that I had an artistic background and that my marriage and kids were, in his words, "very good".

The astrologer continued to smile as he was telling my friend that I have "so many ideas" and am "never satisfied." He gestured a spinning, circular motion with his hands over his head to indicate lots of thoughts, which was pretty remarkable, as I had battled with excessive mind chatter for as long as I could remember. He predicted that would be resolved, and I would be better and more stable starting in 2025 and for the twenty years thereafter. Looking back at the notes I took that day, I see "10/17/18– 10/17/25 I will create based on spirituality." I can't remember the exact details around that phrase, but it certainly resonated. In fact, it couldn't be more accurate.

There were so many amazing experiences like this on the trip, and although it is difficult to choose, I would have to say my favorite experience was the 660-foot hike up the epic ancient rock fortress of Sigiriya. It was an incredibly hot day, but the view from the top, overlooking the surrounding countryside, was worth the heat and so unforgettably picturesque that I chose it for the cover of this book.

Our ten-day spiritual adventure reaffirmed my certainty of miracles. The monks led by example, and being in their presence for over a week was soul-warming. It was amazing to watch how they conducted themselves in public, planning and organizing so many logistics with ease, humor and kindness. We traveled more than five hundred miles. I nearly filled my journal, writing for hours and looking out the window of our bus. The trip was the perfect opportunity to reflect on all that had happened in the past six months. I had new revelations and insights as a result of so many wonderful encounters.

The last excursion in Sri Lanka was to Trincomalee, a port city on the northeast coast. A swim in the sea was the perfect ending, and to top it off, the monks joined our dip in the Indian Ocean! That evening after our celebratory dip, we were sitting around after dinner by the pool that overlooked the beach where we had gone swimming. Someone mentioned to Bhante Samitha that I had donated my kidney to my husband. His

English was limited, but his jolly demeanor and warmth went beyond language, allowing us to communicate. I'll never forget him stoically looking at me and stating clearly, "Thank You". I was profoundly moved that I had acted in a way that generated this response, especially coming from someone whose life's work was giving. In that moment, I truly felt I had come full circle.

# EPILOGUE

I returned home from Sri Lanka feeling like a hero on her hero's journey. I had won the battle against the most challenging opponent, myself. From Sedona to Sri Lanka, I had indeed 'Recovered My True Self'! I took my time settling back into life after returning. When the dust settled, I went back to my writing room with all of my new inspiration and reflected on the trip and the overall journey. I felt deep peace, contentment and gratitude, and yet, I also wondered what was next.

It became very clear to me, now that I had recovered my true self, the next step was to go beyond my own personal journey and become a more conscious citizen. It was then that my spiritual path took a turn to an unexpected place—the campaign trail! On Martin Luther King Day, a few weeks after I came back from Sri Lanka, I discovered that Marianne Williamson had placed her writing, and her A Course in Miracles lecturing career, on hold. She had decided to run as a Democratic nominee for the 2020 presidential race. During her campaign speeches, it felt like Marianne was speaking directly to me. Marianne's campaign, called 'A Politics of Love', would attempt to use the principles of personal transformation—which I, myself, had just experienced first-hand—as tools to help transform a nation. So, even as I was embarking on the writing of my book in the seclusion of my writing room, I made a conscious decision to venture out into the wider world in order to help the Marianne Williamson campaign try to make a difference.

In the meantime, in August 2019, we marked the one-year anniversary of Ken's kidney transplant. He had made a wonderful recovery. His monthly blood work showed normal creatinine, indicating healthy kidney function. The level of the anti-rejection medications sometimes needed minor adjustments, but were more often in the indicated therapeutic range. We were relieved that the side effects from the medications were mild. Occasionally, he would experience headaches, varying from minor to more debilitating. Regardless, his vivacity had returned, and he was back to his usual light hearted, witty, energetic self. He had returned to work two months after the surgery and for the past year had been able to work full time seamlessly. Seeing him return to leisure activities that summer was amazing. Watching him swing a golf club (which had been prohibited for six months due to risk of a hernia or injuring his large inguinal incision), seeing him go fishing off his kayak, or spike a volleyball on the beach, and body surf in the rough ocean waves truly felt miraculous.

That October, as part of Organ Enrollment Day, an event was organized at Ken's hospital. The aim of the event was to raise awareness about the importance of organ donation. Ken and I were asked to share our story and also participate in local media interviews covering the event. The interviews, and the event itself, were a wonderful opportunity for Ken and I to share and reflect on how far we had come. It was wonderful seeing people enjoy our story; they especially loved that we were a match. People enjoyed hearing about Ken's new creative personality traits, which we had no doubt were courtesy of the kidney I had donated to him. It was also moving for us to hear the other presenters share their experiences of giving and receiving organ donations. It was especially emotional to hear stories of the many lives saved—even in the cases of the untimely deaths of the deceased donors. Overall, Organ Enrollment Day was successful in creating a day of action and in getting people to sign up to be organ donors at registerme.org.

November came, and my 39th birthday was approaching. I was juggling my usual load of motherhood, physical therapy work, and volunteering for the Marianne Williamson campaign. It had been almost two years since my initial premonition to write this book. The initial writing of the book was a divine process. The editing and revising, on the other hand, was a much different endeavor—much more of a struggle. Editing definitely proved to be challenging. It didn't help that I found smaller and smaller windows in which to focus on the revisions. I had begun to be more deeply involved in Marianne's campaign, which lasted for another two months.

Marianne was a non-establishment candidate. Her campaign was an uphill battle from the start. Still, she made it to the presidential debate stage and definitely made an impact on the political discourse. Hearing her talk from her unique perspective, felt like the beginning of a paradigm shift. This shift soothed us when the campaign ended in January, right before the Iowa caucuses.

People would ask me why I spent my time supporting a candidate that the polls and media declared had no chance. The naysayers sounded like the egoic voices in my head that had asked, "Who are you to write a book?" For me, as I watched and listened to Marianne speak and interact with people on the campaign trail, it all felt right. I made a conscious choice not to listen to the media, the polls, or the negative voices. When it came to Marianne's campaign, my soul said (as it had when I made the decision to write my book) 'go for it'. Listening to my inner voice brought profound satisfaction and an inner triumph.

As I write this now, in February, 2021, so much more has happened. I have enjoyed living life from this new, divine vantage point, yet challenges still seem to be waiting around each corner. For example, the final editing process leading up to this book's publication took a much longer time than I had expected. As stated earlier, the initial writing was a divine process and a creative purge; it felt good to get it out. It was also healing and therapeutic, so I figured I was done, that the book was ready. The reality was, even though that first draft made me feel complete, there was so much more still to be done.

The seemingly never ending editing process constantly frustrated me, especially given my ego's relentless attachment to arriving at the finish line. Ultimately, as I came to accept the process, I was able to surrender to the realization that the only way out was through. Painfully tedious as editing and revisions often were, when I let go and got out of my own way, I was surprised when once again I felt satisfaction, and even joy. It was also a reminder that I needed to be patient, which is something I have struggled with throughout my life. Any parent will tell you that years of parenting certainly increases one's threshold for patience. It's said, 'good things come to those who wait'. As I patiently toiled along, the good things came— volunteers who assisted me by bringing fresh eyes and fresh perspectives, and family and friends who believed in me and encouraged me—all of it enhancing this book, helping bring it to a place I never thought possible!

There is no question life is more meaningful since my transformational experience, yet I can't deny having to continually remind myself of the lessons I reflect on in this book. Reading and re-reading the book again and again during editing allowed me to reflect on its themes, in particular on perfection and forgiveness. For most of my life, I felt plagued by perfection. After my transformative experience, I shifted from a limiting mindset, from trying to achieve what I call 'human perfection' to an attitude of 'divine perfection'. Going forward, my mission is to continue putting all of this into practice.

This circuitous road of perfection leads ultimately to a destination of forgiveness. I take a deep breath as I reflect and write the word 'forgiveness'—a word that simultaneously triggers and heals. Forgiveness is a big topic. You might say, forgiveness is the art of letting yourself and others off the hook and involves releasing grievances. It is a concept that comes around again and again, each time allowing us to see how forgiveness truly equals freedom. The triggering part comes in the letting go and requires unpacking the luggage of resistance. This process gets a bit ugly at times, but every time around it gets smoother, and ultimately, the alternatives are far worse. There is a lesson in *A Course in Miracles* that states, 'Forgiveness is my function as the light of the world'. I agree.

When I make the mistake of falling victim to the limiting notion of human perfection, it is the process of surrender, and of forgiving myself and others, that leads me back to divine perfection. As I worked on this book's revisions and began the process of publication, I focused on forgiveness at every turn. Finding mistakes, and clarifying thoughts that weren't clear, even after multiple rounds of editing, made me feel hopeless that this book would ever be finished. After the initial sting, the realization would come; I am human, I make mistakes, and I would circle back around to forgiveness. Forgiveness restored my faith and encouraged me to take it one step at a time. As I accepted that my arbitrary timeline was in the realm of human perfection, I was able to soothe my mind with the knowledge that my book would get done on its own divinely perfect timeline.

This past year also brought the COVID-19 Pandemic. It has been a hard and complicated time. But, as unprecedented as this time has been, it has interestingly also brought a feeling of déjà vu. Right after the transplant, Ken was restricted from taking the subway, or being in large crowds and other high germ environments. The pandemic brought these precautions to the public at large and made the term 'social distancing' a new phrase in people's vocabularies. I don't remember the words 'social distancing' actually being used in conjunction with the transplant, but it was essentially what we had to do. Ken was encouraged to be selective in choosing social situations and to consider if socializing was worth the risk. We would ask ahead if people were ill; now during the pandemic, the same was being asked of everyone. When Ken did go out, he was told to carry a small bottle of hand sanitizer with him. I stocked up on Purell to fill and refill the tiny bottles Ken kept in his pocket and in the car and in my purse. Now, during the pandemic, the experts were advising everyone to social distance and to frequently wash their hands. I opened my bathroom linen closet to see the giant bottle of hand sanitizer—now in short supply—I had bought after the transplant. The quiet during the lockdown months felt similar to the solitary months Ken and I experienced after the organ donation. As distressing as it all has been—and was—I can't deny enjoying the peacefulness and the time it has allowed for reflection and the opportunity to be with our children.

The unprecedented part was how the whole country—and the world—were all in lock down as well. The pandemic was something much bigger than just us. It was shocking seeing the empty grocery shelves and upsetting to know of all the struggles people were experiencing. There was also the huge impact of the schools closing. Everything was changing.

The COVID-19 pandemic leaves lots of unknowns ahead, not unlike the unknowns Ken and I faced after the transplant. Yet, the irony of Ken receiving a transplant and being immunocompromised, even as he continued to work at the hospital during a pandemic, highlighted the importance of shifting from a personal journey to one of becoming a conscious citizen. People were struggling, but they were also rising up. It was heartwarming to see handmade rainbows children had made that their parents hung up in the windows of their homes. So too was seeing billboards proudly thanking our 'health care heroes'. Essential workers were collecting our garbage and risking their lives so we could have our basic provisions. This was a paradox—being apart and divided, but also coming together.

The teachings of A Course in Miracles (ACIM), as they did during the transplant, have brought me clarity and helped make sense of these complex times. When dealing with the fear I encounter in my personal life, and in the external world, I realize again and again that I need to surrender my fear to a higher power, rather than simply relying on my own strength. This brings the peaceful feeling of knowing there is a divine power much stronger and more capable than I am, a power I can always trust and rely on. Studying the daily teachings in the ACIM workbook has been abundantly helpful. This year, more than ever, I pray for a miracle—which the Course defines as a shift from fear to love. The miracles surrounding the transplant are my proof, every day, of the power of love, which is always there to uplift me during difficult and challenging times.

I have experienced tremendous healing in the writing of this book. I go forward with brave faith and spiritual perseverance. It has been an amazing journey, and I would like to end with these words from Ester Hicks: 'I am incredibly satisfied, and eager for more'!

Wishing you all peace and blessings on your journey and praying that we continue to come together to elevate the consciousness of humanity.

March 15, 2021
Hampton Bays, NY

# TOOLBOX

As I said at the beginning, this is not a self-help book designed to tell you how to fix your broken life. Therefore, none of these things listed below are intended to 'fix' you (except maybe for meditation). However, if you do feel like you are looking for direction, or are in a rut, here are some suggestions. As Esther Hicks says, "The better you feel, the more you allow."

These tools are listed in no particular order. Having said that, I did put meditation first, as I truly believe it is the most effective and powerful. Give these tools a go. If one doesn't work, try a new one and then go back to the other again. Try not to get frustrated if you are not doing it perfectly—as I often do—just keep going with your inner voice as the guide!

When the void shows up—mine comes later in the day, and especially when I'm tired, hungry, over stimulated and overwhelmed—I try to fill it with one of these tools instead of using food, alcohol and other void fillers. Hello, media! These tools aren't always a quick fix, but they can be quite effective. If the momentum of whatever you are dealing with is too strong, my best advice is to remove yourself from the situation. Find a way to push the internal reset button by taking a walk or taking a nap. A deep breath, connection with spirit, surrendering, or a prayer can also help in a pinch. Give yourself a pat on the back for acknowledging the resistance and the void—even if you don't fill it perfectly. And of course, none of this is intended to replace traditional medical diagnosis and treatment but rather to be used in conjunction.

## Meditation

I can't emphasize this one enough! For years, I thought I didn't have enough time to meditate. Now, if I don't meditate, I don't have enough clarity to remember what my time is for. I prefer fifteen minutes in the morning before the day gets away from me. On a good day, I try to get a second shorter meditation in after lunch or in the evening. I must admit that getting the second one in is often a challenge. If I meditated more consistently in the evenings, perhaps my evenings would pose less of a challenge.

In an effort to release the compulsion for perfection, or if I accidentally sleep in or am running late—getting the kids to school for example—I fit my morning meditation in somewhere else. Meditation is a remedy when my head starts to spin. When the kids are out of school and my regimen is challenged, I settle for stopping a few times throughout the day. I go to my room and lie on my bed and reconnect with my breath and Spirit. I find the real key is stopping, even if just for a few moments, wherever I happen to be.

Meditation is the place to go when you don't know what to do. It connects you with your inner voice which knows exactly what to do. We live in a noisy world. Meditation helps quiet the external noise and transcend the ego. It is a place where the divine and the inner self speak and can be heard. The healing and reconnection, to yourself and to Spirit, that occurs during meditation can be quite profound and also relaxing.

There are many different techniques, but meditation is basically sitting or lying down and resting. There are various techniques that will refine and enhance your practice, but if you can stop, sit and breathe, you are 90 percent there. There are also wonderful apps that can assist you. Do not get frustrated if you have a million thoughts racing by. The point is not to get rid of them; it is to stop identifying with them.

## A Course in Miracles

The sheer size of this giant blue textbook is intimidating, but the name says it all. It is a self-study course in the allowing of miracles. The book is divided into three sections: the text, a workbook for students with 365 daily lessons, and a manual for teachers. In the introduction it states, 'This is a course in miracles. It is a required course. Only the time you take it is voluntary'. I had heard the book referenced many times throughout the years, and when it unexpectedly appeared in my mailbox, I knew it was my time. I have been studying *A Course in Miracles* for a few years now, and, for me, I know it will be a lifelong study. You may want to get the book and put it on your bookshelf for when it may be your time. It is not a light read, but the contents are life changing.

## Exercise

If you Google 'the benefits of exercise', you will get a nice list of things that you are probably aware of. My favorite benefit is feeling happier. Most people who exercise will agree, and I certainly do. Walking and yoga are my favorites, but the best exercises are the ones that you will actually do! If you are just starting out or resuming an exercise program, be mindful to start slowly.

When exercising, it is a bonus if you can find a way to work in an errand or make a phone call you have been intending to make. I get such a kick when I take a bike ride and manage to run an errand in town, or take a walk and catch up with a friend I have been meaning to call. If you are going to the gym, maybe you can stop along the way to mail a letter. The best part is coming home and crossing items off your to-do list. Instead of meeting a friend for lunch, go for a walk together. The conversations that occur during walks are way better, and they are free from calories and dollars!

## Yoga

There is a reason people have been practicing yoga for more than five thousand years. I, myself, have practiced yoga for more than twenty years. I completed my two hundred-hour teacher training in 2009. There are many different types of yoga practice. From my experience, I have learned it's not about the type of yoga you do, it's that you do it.

Yoga can change your life on so many levels: physically, mentally, and spiritually. Don't take my word for it, try it, and then try it again and again in whatever capacity works for you. Take a class at the studio down the street, and if you don't like it, go again with a different teacher, or try a different studio. See if your local library offers yoga classes. When you are away from home or out of town, try it there. There are also yoga DVDs, as well as many online platforms, including YouTube.

If you are struggling with an injury, check with your doctor or physical therapist and also tell your yoga instructor prior to class. Lately, my writing has taken a lot of my yoga time, so instead of going to my favorite classes and studios, I have been enjoying a fifteen or twenty-minute home practice. Yoga isn't for everyone, but it is definitely worth taking the time to give it a try.

## Artist Date

I started going on Artist Dates while undergoing the creative recovery process described in *The Artist Way*, by Julia Cameron. The concept of the Artist Date is discussed in detail in Cameron's book and also at JuliaCameronlive.com. Basically, it is a once-weekly, festive solo expedition to explore something that interests you. It is often helpful to get away from your desk and look for fresh insights and perspectives in the world around you.

My weekly Artist's Dates would sometimes consist of the more obvious artistic ventures, such as visits to local museums and going to musical performances. Other times, my Artist Dates would include visiting places that were not overtly artistic, such as a new hiking trail, a drive to a town I had never been to, or a visit to a shop I had driven by multiple times and was curious about. It was satisfying to feed my curiosity. Making the effort to connect was inspirational and allowed me to see the creativity all around me. As Cameron puts it, 'Artist Dates spark whimsy' and 'encourage play'. I agree. I encourage you to give it a try. When choosing an Artist Date, ask yourself, "What sounds fun?", and allow yourself to try it.

## Psychotherapy

I am a strong advocate for paying attention to mental health. I often call therapy a 'massage for your brain'. Going to therapy doesn't mean you are broken, nor does it mean you are weak; it means you want to fix what's holding you back in order to be the best version of yourself. It takes courage to get help. Talking in a safe, supportive environment is essential. It doesn't necessarily have to occur in a therapist's office; conversations about what is going on with you can occur in other places, such as support groups and with close family and friends.

An objective and professional environment is often necessary to truly get outside your comfort zone and do the work of going deep down underneath the superficial symptoms. Depending on your individual preferences and needs, there are many types of therapy available. I myself have seen two different licensed clinical social workers (LCSW). I wouldn't be where I am today without therapy, and I am so grateful for the two therapists I worked with. I'm so glad I got past feeling insulted when, years ago, my graduate school advisor referred me to counseling. To this day, I still keep in touch with the therapists I worked with.

My first therapist was a LCSW who did more traditional psychotherapy. The other was a LCSW who incorporated holistic therapies including: Reiki, essential oils, breath work, hypnotherapy and meditation. You can check online or in your community for referrals. Your health insurance company might be able to help you. Plus, there is a growing trend of health insurance companies that cover the cost of therapy. Yes, there is often an out-of-pocket expense, but how much is your mental health worth?

## Energy Therapy

In addition to psychotherapies, there are also energy therapies. Many people believe that healers can channel healing energy. This is a broad category that includes: Reiki, craniosacral therapy, spiritual response therapy and Tong Ren, amongst others. It's not really fair to lump these various therapies together; there are differences. It is usually best to contact and connect with the practitioner to learn about his, or her, unique background, training and specialty.

Energy work can often be done distantly, which is quite convenient. I have had many sessions done over the phone with lots of amazing results. These therapies are often criticized by skeptics, but having been on the receiving end, I say they are totally worth a shot! You have little to lose and lots to gain.

The biggest benefit is they allow you to experience the power of intention. If you set aside time to work with a healer and intend to get better, often you do. There is a ton of information out there on the specifics of these therapies and how they work. Another benefit is connecting you with your own inner healing abilities. Reiki practitioners will quickly attune

161

the individual to do the work on themselves. Healers don't necessarily have special powers that others don't; they are just often very connected in areas where others have become disconnected. Being in the presence of a healer who is connected will reconnect you, and before long, you may become your own healer.

## Essential Oils

Concentrated oils from plants are widely available. Oils have wonderful therapeutic benefits and can be uplifting or calming and have an instant effect on your vibration. They are fun to sample and experiment with—so give it a shot! Go to your local health food store and smell, diffuse and research.

There is plenty of information out there to get started on your own. There are disagreements about which companies produce the highest-quality oils. There is also the decision of organic versus nonorganic. Different countries have different plant-growing standards and restrictions on chemical pesticides. Since they are so concentrated, quality is important. These oils are quite powerful and should be used as directed. Be careful with pets, read the labels, and research the companies to ensure they are good quality—especially if you are using them around your kids.

## Healing Crystals

My sister turned me on to these a while back. They are beautiful to look at, and they can aid in healing. I love looking at the larger crystals on my desk; they inspire me when I am working. When I am feeling overstimulated, I hold a smaller crystal—which I keep in my pocket or my purse—to help me feel more grounded. Crystals look beautiful when worn as jewelry, which is a wonderful dual purpose: beauty and healing. Crystals are also available in metaphysical shops, yoga studios, health food stores and online websites. The places that sell them usually give out information on the specific benefits of the various crystals. There are a lot of books written on the benefits of crystals and plenty of information can be found on the internet.

## Herbal Supplements/Homeopathy

There are all sorts of herbal combinations that promote health and wellness. They come in capsules, sprays, and drops for under your tongue. The National Center for Homeopathy says homeopathy is a safe, gentle and natural system of healing that works with your body to restore itself and improve your overall health. Herbal supplements and homeopathy have helped me, and I recommend giving them a try.

The body has a greater affinity for wellness than disease and sometimes just needs assistance and faith. Herbs and supplements are available online and at health food shops and are worth exploring. Perhaps they don't work as quickly as pharmaceuticals, but they can enhance your body's natural ability to heal itself. There are also wonderful herbalists and naturopaths who will diagnose and treat specific conditions with herbs. Don't throw away your medication and replace it with herbs—and always check with your doctor.

## Visualization

For many years, I associated visualization techniques with meditation. At the end of yoga classes, teachers often turn down the lights and lead the group into the glorious deep restorative corpse pose, or in Sanskrit 'Savasana'. Each teacher has their own style, but a common thread is to visualize white light moving through each part of the body in order to relax and release it.

Esther Hicks uses a term called 'pre-paving' to visualize how you want upcoming situations to manifest. As my meditation practice has evolved over the years, I have combined a lot of these techniques. In *Being at Your Best When Your Kids Are at Their Worst,* Kim John Payne articulates it even better. Payne discusses how young athletes in Australia work with sports psychologists who teach them visualization techniques to inwardly picture themselves performing optimally prior to playing their sport.

Before I get out of bed in the morning, I imagine myself doing the small steps of getting ready, picking out clothes, preparing breakfast and getting my kids off to school with ease and love. I'm not going to say it happens 100 percent perfectly every time, but it sets the intention for how I want things to go. Using visualization, I am being proactive instead of reactive. I use it for the more ordinary aspects of life and the grander visions.

When facing difficult situations, often fear creeps in, and I find myself thinking about failure before it even occurs. Once I realize this, I pray for a miracle, which is the shift from fear to love. Pre-paving and visualizing the situation through a lens of love gets you out in front. You are telling the universe what you want instead of attracting what you don't want. I find it empowering and am often amazed at how well these situations go when I do this work. Try it—and you will be amazed!

Last but not least, it is important to remember to unplug and tune into you! Turn off the TV and your devices and breathe, then read! I frequent the library and take out lots of books. I don't always finish them all, but when I find something in a book that resonates with me, I write it down and celebrate! I feel like I am finding clues that the universe has hidden for me. It is like a treasure hunt. As I feel the synchronicity on the pages before me, I thank God and the author for such wonderful revelations.

I hope that at least some of these techniques will be helpful to you. Most importantly have the courage to tell your story—we want to hear it!

# REFERENCES

Cameron, J. (2016). *The Artist's Way: The 25ᵗʰ Anniversary Edition. New York:* Tarcher Perigee.

Dyer, W. (2015). *I Can See Clearly Now.* Carlsbad: Hay House.

Salmansohn, K. (2001). *How to Be Happy, Dammit.* Berkeley: Celestial Arts.

Tolle, E. (2001). *Practicing the Power of Now.* Novato: New World Library.

Payne, K. (2009). *Simplicity Parenting.* New York: Ballantine Books.

Oppenheimer, S. (2006). *Heaven on Earth.* Great Barrington: Steiner Books.

Dancy, R. (2012). *You Are Your Child's First Teacher.* Berkeley: Celestial Arts.

Hay, L. (1984). *You Can Heal Your Life.* Carlsbad: Hay House.

Hicks, E & J. (2004). *Ask and It Is Given.* Carlsbad: Hay House.

Gilbert, E. (2016). *Big Magic.* New York: Riverhead Books.

*A Course in Miracles*: Combined Volume (3ʳᵈ Edition). (2007). Mill Valley: Foundation for Inner Peace.

Sylvia, C. (1997). *A Change of Heart: A Memoir.* New York: Little Brown.

Orloff, J. (2018). *Empath Survival Guide.* Louisville: Sound True.

Aron, Elaine. (1997). *The Highly Sensitive Person.* New York: Broadway Books.

Pressfield, S. (2012). *The War of Art.* Black Irish Books.

Ortner, J. (2014). *Tapping for Weight Loss.* Carlsbad: Hay House.

Melton, G. (2016). *Love Warrior.* New York: Flatiron Books.

Ruiz, D. (1997). *The Four Agreements.* San Rafael: Amber-Allen Publishing.

Luskin, F. (2003). *Forgive for Good.* San Francisco: Harper One.

Payne, K. (2019). *Being at Your Best When Your Kids Are at Their Worst.* Boulder: Shambhala.

# ACKNOWLEDGMENTS

For many years, I have overlooked the acknowledgment page in so many books. However, since I started writing this book it is often the first page I read. The reason for this change is because now that I have experienced the book writing process, I see that I could never have done it alone. Therefore, this page has never felt more significant to me. I want to give a big thank you from the bottom of my heart to the wonderful people in my life who have supported, challenged and played with me.

To my husband, Ken, who has supported me literally every step I have taken and allowed me to feel unconditional love. Without it, I would never have experienced this extraordinary journey that we call our life. Thank you for the endless hours of listening to my ranting, raving and everything in between. I'd give you every organ in my body in exchange for all you have done for me, and I will always believe that we are 'a perfect match'.

To my children, for reconnecting me with my own inner child, for allowing me to discover the most meaningful work life has to offer, and for inspiring my creative journey. You show me how creativity is truly something we are born with, and as I watch you create, I am in awe. I love you to the moon and back.

As I stated in the dedication, thank you to my mother for bringing me into this world. I never could have created this life, or this book, without you.

To my dad for teaching me about life's infinite possibilities—this book was certainly one of them—and for paving the way of how to live as a nonconformist.

To Allison, thank you for being my soul sister and lifelong partner in crime.

To the rest of my wonderful extended family and friends for your love and support; although I can't name each and every one of you, you know who you are.

To Michael Mullins, this book would definitely not be in this version without you. I am so deeply grateful for your friendship, which evolved into a divine partnership. Thank you for believing in me and in this book and for the endless hours of your time you volunteered to edit this book and help transform it into a version I never thought possible. You lead by example and show me how to live gracefully and fabulously.

To my healers: Ruth, Lois, Kristie, Tracey, Julie, the astrologer in Sri Lanka, and the psychic in Sedona. I thank you for your unwavering service and subsequent synchronicity.

To Aunt Sandy for the journals. You probably had no idea I would fill all of them!

To the authors I reference in this book. Thank you for the path you paved for me. I am especially grateful to Marianne Williamson and the late Louise Hay, their work has inspired and guided me throughout the process of writing this book.

I want to acknowledge Lisa and Susan for taking the time to read this manuscript and offering their valuable insights.

I also want to thank you, the reader. It took a long time, and a lot of courage, to get here, and I thank you deeply for allowing me to share my story with you.

Made in the USA
Las Vegas, NV
09 June 2021